THE
JILL ST. JOHN
COOKBOOK

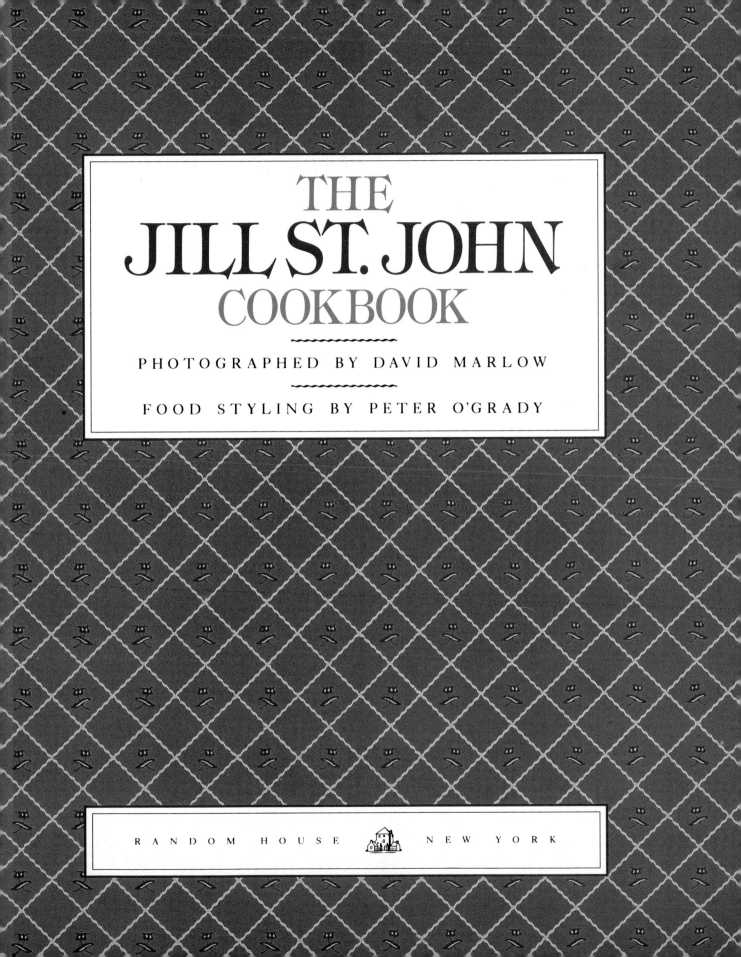

THE JILL ST. JOHN COOKBOOK

PHOTOGRAPHED BY DAVID MARLOW

FOOD STYLING BY PETER O'GRADY

RANDOM HOUSE · NEW YORK

Many of the recipes in this book first appeared in *USA Weekend.*®
Copyright © 1985, 1986, 1987 *USA Weekend.*

Library of Congress Cataloging-in-Publication Data

St. John, Jill.
The Jill St. John cookbook.

Includes index.
1. Cookery.   I. Title.
TX715.S7745 1987   641.5   87-12721
ISBN 0-394-56132-5

Manufactured in the United States of America

2   3   4   5   6   7   8   9

First Edition

DESIGN BY JOEL AVIROM

~~~~~~~~~~

This book is dedicated to the memory of Lance,
who taught me almost everything I know,
in or out of the kitchen.

~~~~~~~~~~

I would like to express my gratitude to the Eastman Kodak Company, which provided EKTACHROME 64 and 100 Professional Films and arranged for the processing of these films for the illustrations in my book, as well as invaluable technical advice. You probably never associated Kodak with cooking. I know I didn't. But when my photographer, David Marlow, and I tested films from a number of manufacturers, we found that the Kodak films most accurately captured the rich colors and textures of my creations. I couldn't have completed this book nearly as well without their help. Thanks, Kodak!

ACKNOWLEDGMENTS

My thanks to the cast and crew. With my background in film, the easiest way for me to plan the photography for this book was to lay it out as though I were producing and directing a movie. On paper I laid out each individual photograph as though it were a scene in a movie. I would first check the availability of ingredients, so as to have the freshest possible. Then I would choose the location for the day's shoot. We might shoot in one place all day, or all week, depending on our needs. I would then schedule the photographs according to the length of time needed to prepare the various dishes. Armed with this time schedule, I was then able to begin the art direction. This meant choosing furniture, flowers, linens, china, candles, silver, props and accessories of all kinds to enhance our chosen backgrounds, or sets, as I call them. I planned an eighteen-day shoot. We stayed on schedule (working twelve-hour days). We had to, as fresh foods were arriving daily to coincide with our shooting schedule. It was a mammoth undertaking and could only have been accomplished by true professionals.

The entire book was conceived and executed in Aspen,

by Aspenites. *David Marlow*, our great photographer, was my first and only choice to photograph this book. A brilliant commercial photographer, David has also shot two of my favorite portraits of myself, one for the cover of *Aspen* magazine, the other for the cover of *Electricity*. These two great working experiences, plus a glimpse of David's portfolio, convinced me that his considerable talent as well as his great disposition would help make the project successful. David and his assistant, *Steve Mundinger*, never let us down.

Peter O'Grady, owner of Creative Catering, was our food stylist and caterer. Peter never failed to prepare the food in such decorative and delectable ways that we almost hated to eat it. I say almost because in three weeks we ate the entire cookbook. Peter does a lot of the food styling for my column in *USA Weekend*. *Paul "P.J." Johnston*, Peter's assistant and my old camping buddy, provided not only his talent but his great good nature. The way P.J. can cook and bake over a campfire is a book in itself.

Another Aspenite, *Darlene Vare*, assisted me with the art direction. It was Darlene who found all the wonderful napkin rings, vases, candlesticks, laces, gloves, and so on. Darlene pulled it together. If we needed something, she found it and made it work. A stylist for *Mademoiselle* and other New York fashion magazines, Darlene has also written for *Vogue* and *Cuisine*. Darlene also introduced me to *Mike Garrish*. Mike is a former mayor of Aspen who now spends a great deal of time gardening. He generously gave me a pair of scissors and allowed me to cut whatever I needed. He even let me cut part of his raspberry patch. The hothouse flowers, and all the trees you will see, came from the *Lazy Glen Greenhouse and Nursery*. I've been buying plants and trees from them for fifteen years and have now come to think of Lazy Glen as the home of my money.

My secretary and personal assistant, *Sally Sherman*, is just as valued as the rest of the crew. Sally had the unenviable job of unpacking and keeping track of thirty-nine boxes of crystal and china from Villeroy and Boch, boxes of linens from Paper White, and all the other tableware and props that we used. Nothing was lost or broken, and that's due to Sally.

My grateful thanks are also due to Karen Keane, who worked long hours at Stuart-Buchanan Antiques so that we could photograph there as late as necessary; Glenn Frey, George Giannini and Carolanne Charles, who lent their gorgeous china, crystal and silver; Dick Sturgis, Laura Donnelley, Jack and Lou, who lent their beautiful houses; and, of course, the staffs of the Jerome Hotel, Wax and Wicks, Best of All Worlds, Patricia Moore, Inc., Les Chefs D'Aspen, Special Occasions and Lazy Glen Nursery. Thanks everybody. You were great!

There are two companies that have graciously loaned me their beautiful products so that I might photograph my recipes in the most attractive settings. *Villeroy and Boch* provided the magnificent china and crystal patterns that are scattered throughout this book. I've owned their Indian Summer and Petite Fleur patterns for years. Seeing all those lovely patterns has made me hungry for more. As magnificent as all the Villeroy and Boch china is, I feel it reached its full beauty sitting on top of the incredible lacy linens from *Paper White*. All of the white tablecloths, napkins, pillows and bed linens are from Paper White. In particular, the photographs of me in bed with a breakfast tray are a perfect example of the variety and versatility of these incredible linens. No matter how good food tastes, when presented on such beautiful china and linens, it truly seems to taste better.

To say thanks to all of the wonderful friends who graciously loaned their nicest tableware, linens, quilts, furniture and flowers is to take you on a walking tour of the best shops in Aspen. One of the advantages of living in a small town is that you end up knowing most people—and in my case, some of the nicest people. Let me figuratively walk you through our town. We start on Main and Mill, at the magnificent *Jerome Hotel*. Built in 1893 at the height of the silver boom, it was lovingly restored to its original Victorian grandeur by its present owner, Dick Butera. Dick was generous to a fault in allowing us to photograph in all of the gorgeous public and private rooms. Walk two blocks up Mill Street to Hyman Avenue, turn left and walk for one block, and stop in at *Wax and Wicks*, a most unique candle and candlestick store. Turn left when you leave, and continue walking along Hyman past Galena and Hunter streets. A few more steps and you're at *Patricia Moore, Inc.* My dear friend Pat Moore has

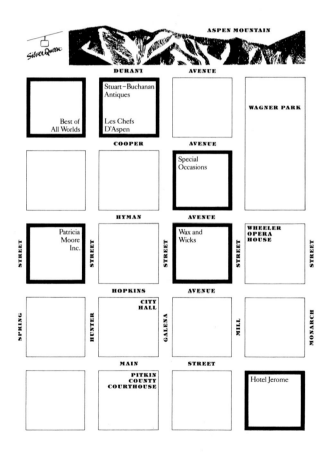

had a great housewares-gift shop ever since 1954. Besides her great selection of gifts, from silver frames to wooden spoons, and from ceramic mugs to crystal vases, Pat has a terrific selection of cookbooks. I know, because for years I was her cookbook consultant. You can imagine how proud I am to have this book on sale at her wonderful store. When you leave Pat's, turn right at her door, go to the corner, Hunter Street, make a left and go one block to Cooper Avenue. Make a left on Cooper, walk a few more steps, and you are now at *Best of All Worlds*. True to its name, Best of All Worlds provided us with beautiful tableware and accessories from many countries. Turn left when leaving and walk back to the corner of Hunter Street and Cooper Avenue. You are now at *Les Chefs D'Aspen*, where so many of the utensils, pans, pots and pottery I used came from. Besides any cooking utensil you could think of, they also have a cooking school. Their guest teachers have included Jacques Pépin, Giuliano Bugialli and Wolfgang Puck. Turn left when you leave Les Chefs D'Aspen and go a block and a half. On the opposite side of Cooper Avenue is *Special Occasions*, owned by my friend Lita Heller, and it is exactly that, a shop where you buy gifts for special occasions. So many of the lovely things photographed with my recipes are from

Special Occasions, including Lita's fine French and Italian silverware. When you leave, turn left and walk half a block to Cooper and Mill. Go right on Mill to Durant Avenue and one and a half blocks to the left will bring you to *Stuart-Buchanan Antiques*. All of the stunning French country antiques we photographed are from Stuart-Buchanan, whose decorator, Royce Colon, coordinated all those yummie armoires, tables and chairs, not to mention the incredible collection of antique quilts from *Katie Ingham* that are on sale there. Katie has been supplying Aspenites with her collection of rare and fine quilts for years. I spray mine with a dirt and moisture resistant and use them as tablecloths. Go back to Mill Street and walk three blocks back to the Jerome Hotel bar. Have a Coffee Keoki and marvel at how nice Aspenites are and what a beautiful place they are lucky enough to live in.

INTRODUCTION

I'm not a trained cook. I'm just a person who loves to cook. I've cooked most of my life, but so have a lot of us. I started cooking when I was eight years old. This is not surprising, since I had already started acting by the age of four. To me, how dishes were made was almost as fascinating as "how acting was done." I used to watch old Marlene Dietrich movies on television and marvel that this glamorous woman could make movies by day, and then arrive on the set the next day with strudel and soup that she had made the night before for the cast and crew. At least that's what it said in the movie magazines, and I believe it to this day. I'm still passionate about acting and cooking and am very fortunate to be active in both careers.

Just as actors are not the only facet of acting, cooking is not just about food. What you cook for people can show how you feel about them and yourself. It's not just the time and effort spent preparing your meals that counts; what counts most is preparing healthful, balanced and, of course, delicious meals.

Some of these recipes can be made in twenty to thirty minutes; a few are all-day extravaganzas. Some contain no salt or fat (and don't forget that salt may be deleted from any of my recipes). However, not all of them are so pure. After all, I'm only human. What you will find is a good mixture of dishes that you can use together or separately to fit your own dietary requirements. I don't, however, know anyone whose diet requires my pasta carbonara, but go on, try it. After all, you're only human too. It's the recipe that got me my job as one of the cooking experts on *Good Morning America*. Julia Child was doing a series on celebrity cooks for the show, and I was asked to appear. I honor Julia Child and I was thrilled to meet her. I was

pretty scared to cook anything for this great lady. As you know, her voice is rather high. I was so nervous, mine went up an octave or so, and we sounded like two parakeets. At any rate, the pasta carbonara was a success. The mail was overwhelming and they kept asking me back. So now I am a member of the *Good Morning America* family. *USA Today* covered my debut as the show's newest member, and I am now a food editor for their Sunday magazine, *USA Weekend*.

Both positions expose me to all sorts of cuisine, but it is my acting career and the travel that comes with it that has really broadened my culinary horizons. I seem to be on the move constantly, and in my travels I have dined at some of the world's great restaurants. I offer my own interpretations of some of the great dishes I have enjoyed. My versions are humble by comparison, but with apologies to the great master chefs, I offer them to you. I have also collected recipes from all over the world and have adapted them for American kitchens and ingredients.

Most of the other recipes are made just the way I cook, which is possible because of the way I shop. I plan my menu at the market, utilizing what is freshest that day. This means that I market often, three or four times a week, but I happen to enjoy it. I also spend less money that way. Rather than plan a week's meals in advance, I try to keep certain "must haves" always in my kitchen: butter, olive oil, onions, garlic, tomatoes, a lemon, some potatoes, cheese (any cheese), parsley, a few fresh herbs (I grow my own in pots), some leftover wine, rice, pasta and noodles. With these essentials, plus a piece of fish, fowl or meat, and a fresh vegetable or salad, you can create a feast.

To grow fresh herbs in your garden or on your windowsill, simply pot up plants bought at your garden center or start from seed, using small pots to start. A bag of potting mix will be enough for three or four small pots. Start with the basics—chives, basil, thyme, and so on; you can add more later. Herbs are heavy feeders and enjoy monthly applications of 30–10–10 fertilizer or fish emulsion.

Keep your herbs in a sunny place. Trim off the outer leaves for use, so that you always have some left. Cut the chives straight across, and they will grow back very fast. You can learn glorious ways to use herbs, dried or fresh, not only directly in your cook pot or pan, but to flavor oils, vinegars, salts, pepper mixtures and more. Herbs, spices and a few other things will flavor cheeses and vodkas. I'll also tell you about using edible flowers in salads and side dishes. Along with herb and flower butters, I use all of the flavored oils, vinegars, salts, peppers and extracts in my recipes. You can too, if you like. They're very easy to make and use, and the taste is incredible.

To finish your dinners, I offer several coffee mixtures flavored in the most unusual ways, with cinnamon, vanilla, cardamom, anise and more. I also tell you how to package all of these delicacies, and more, to give as gifts. A bottle of garlic- and herb-flavored oil or vinegar is much more original than a bottle of wine as a bread-and-butter gift, don't you think? At Christmastime, I now get requests from friends for "another jar of my *chèvre* in herbed oil" or "more herbed oil, please." I make up baskets of foods I know my friends enjoy, the most important ingredient being love.

I've never liked cookbooks that tell you what to do without telling you why. If I ask you to mix a little of the hot sauce you have been stirring on the stove into some egg yolks beaten with a little lemon juice, before returning it to the hot sauce on the stove, you will be informed that this is to prevent the sauce from curdling. Hot milk added to mashed potatoes prevents lumps, cold milk makes them like glue. If you overwork pastry dough, it gets tough. Most all of my recipes contain some useful information like that.

If you want your kitchen to be most economical, budget- and timewise, I recommend never throwing anything away! I'm not talking about leftovers. We all know about them, and I'll share with you some of my favorite leftover magic. For example, here's what to do with those dried herbs you've had on the shelf for longer than you care to mention: Toss liberal teaspoonsful of five or six of these "dead herbs" into a large pot of boiling water. Now add garlic, oil and vinegar, and boil artichokes in the aromatic water. Delicious, and because of the oil, the artichokes can be served without butter or mayonnaise.

What I am really talking about, though, are the bones and carcasses from cooked or uncooked meats, fish and fowl. And when you peel your veggies, save the peelings, tops and stems. They are great for the compost pile, but a whole lot better and a lot more immediately rewarding combined with those bones to make the basis for a fabulous steaming bowl of soup. Shrimp and lobster shells . . . are you kidding? These throwaways are the beginnings of great soups and a few sauces. If you are not able to use them now, freeze them for later use. I have a "soup corner" in my freezer consisting of a lot of clear plastic bags filled with these forgotten treasures. I also freeze, in one-cup portions, various soup stocks, as well as the liquids in which I've cooked vegetables. They make great sauces and new soup bases. Unless you're making a soup specifically of cauliflower, broccoli or brussels sprouts, though, don't use their trimmings, as the strong flavor will overpower your stock. Although cabbage is a member of the same (cole) family, I don't mind it in small amounts. Premeasured and oh-so-convenient, these stocks are ever so much better than the store-bought kind. I confess that the "soup corner" of my freezer looks pretty weird, but who besides family looks in your freezer anyway?

Above all, experiment. I have never felt that recipes must be followed exactly. Anyone can be a good cook, given the right recipe and proper ingredients. But a great cook is one who can make do with what he or she has on hand. If I say to use dill and you have only parsley, don't let that stop you. Of course, the two herbs taste different, but both impart a good, distinctive flavor to the food. You can substitute many other herbs for one another: fresh tarragon, sage, rosemary and basil are usually interchangeable. Try them instead of parsley, too. And if you're cutting back on salt in your diet, fresh herbs with a squeeze of lemon will add a great flavor boost to foods —but you already knew that, didn't you? And feel free to substitute margarine or olive oil, or half butter-half olive oil, for the butter I use, whichever seems appropriate.

I love to cook, as I love to eat. In fact, I don't completely trust people who don't like to eat. I think they lack a certain lust for life. But you know I'm not talking about you. Didn't you buy this book so you could try my cooking?

Gifts to & from Your Kitchen

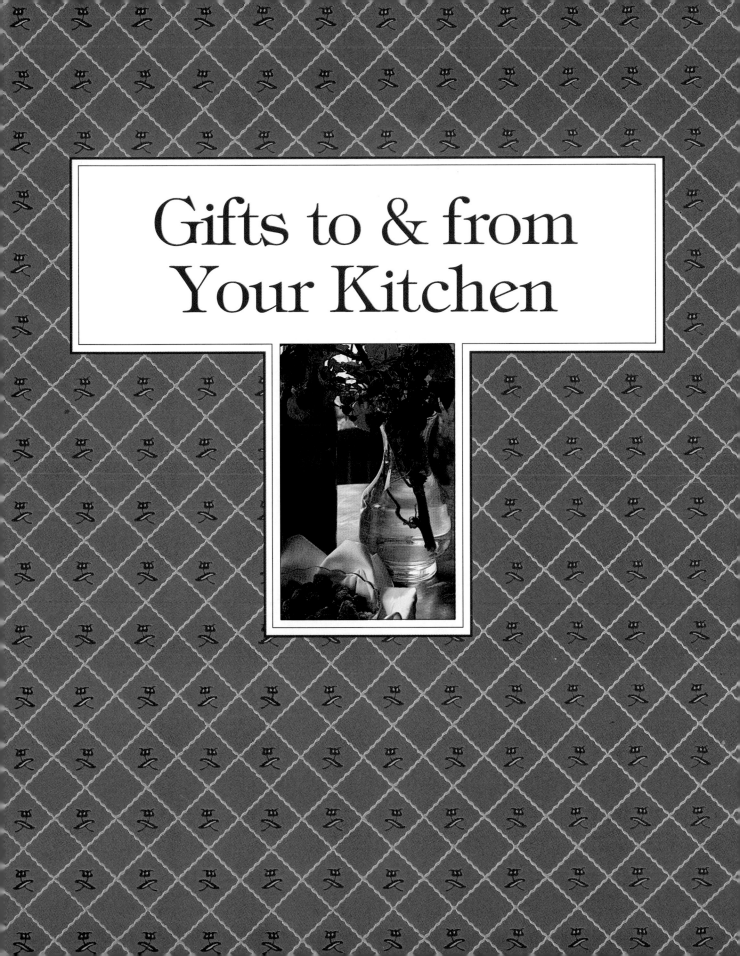

I started out making these "gifts" for myself. Since I grow my own herbs in Colorado, harvest time leaves me with a surplus. I began by infusing olive oils and vinegars with them, then added aromatics such as garlic, ginger, shallots, peppercorns and chili peppers. The resulting oils were so varied and flavorful that I used them exclusively in my cooking and salads. Gradually I expanded my repertoire to include making jellies, cheeses, marmalades, pepper mixtures and so on. These homemade goodies were so popular with my guests that I started making extras to give as bread-and-butter presents when invited to a friend's house for dinner. Personal gifts of food are always greatly appreciated. I now take requests.

Crème de Menthe Jelly, Jalapeño Red Pepper Jelly, Ginger Marmalade, and Herbed-Flavored Oils and Vinegars

Crème de Menthe Jelly

Makes 4 half-pint jars

2 cups fresh peppermint leaves,
stemmed, washed and dried
2 cups water
3⅔ cups sugar
3 tablespoons white wine vinegar
3 ounces liquid pectin
2 tablespoons green crème de menthe
1 or 2 drops green food coloring

Finely chop the mint by hand. (Don't use a food processor, as it tends to purée the leaves, which will make a cloudy jelly.) Put the chopped mint in a medium saucepan, add the water, and place over medium heat. Stir the mixture occasionally until it comes to a boil. Remove the saucepan from the heat, cover and let steep for 15 to 20 minutes. Strain the mint mixture through a sieve that has been lined with a cheesecloth rinsed to remove any detergent residue. (Don't press the mint with a spoon, as that can also make cloudy jelly.) You should have about 1¾ cups liquid. Place the mint liquid, sugar and vinegar in a large saucepan and bring to a boil over high heat. Stir often to dissolve the sugar. When the mixture is at a rolling boil—when it boils to the point that you cannot stir it down—stir in the liquid pectin. Boil for 1 minute. Remove the saucepan from the heat and stir in the crème de menthe and food coloring. Skim off any foam and pour into hot, dry, sterilized canning jars, leaving ¼-inch headspace in each jar. Seal according to manufacturer's directions.

Serve with lamb.

The jelly will keep, sealed, for 6 to 8 months.

Jalapeño Red Pepper Jelly

When working with any kind of hot chili peppers, certain precautions must be observed. Wear rubber gloves when handling them. You will appreciate this advice if you have a cut on your finger, and *never* wipe your eyes. (It really burns.) If you mince the chilis in a food processor, be careful not to inhale the fumes. If you don't take my advice about the gloves, at least wash your hands thoroughly with soap afterward and remember, don't touch your eyes! *Makes about 3 half-pint jars*

1½ cups white cider vinegar
5 cups white sugar
6 raw jalapeño chili peppers, cored, seeded and cut into small pieces
2 red bell peppers, cored, seeded and cut into 1-inch pieces
⅛ teaspoon dried crushed red pepper
3 or 4 drops red food coloring
6 ounces liquid pectin

In a large, heavy pot, bring the vinegar and sugar to a boil, stirring, over low heat. In the work bowl of a food processor fitted with a steel blade, chop the chilis and the red bell peppers—on, off, on, off—until you have a coarse mixture. Do not purée. (You can also chop them by hand, but it will take longer, and you must be careful of the chilis.) When the vinegar and sugar mixture has come to a boil, stir in the chopped peppers and the dried red pepper. Lower the heat and allow to simmer, skimming frequently, for 10 minutes. Add the red food coloring. Stir in the liquid pectin, raise the heat and boil hard for 1 minute. Remove the pan from the heat, skim, and pour into hot, dry, sterilized canning jars, leaving ¼-inch headspace in each jar. Seal according to manufacturer's directions.

Place the sealed jars in a boiling water bath, covering them by at least 1½ inches of water. Cover and boil for 10 minutes. Remove jars with tongs. Cool, label and date. This jelly will keep, sealed, for 6 to 8 months.

Jalapeño red pepper jelly is good with jack cheese as an hors d'oeuvre. The jelly may also be served with meat or chicken.

Instant Raspberry Vinegar

The classic recipe for raspberry vinegar takes several days to complete. My method is definitely cheating. Raspberry vinegar is great for deglazing sauté pans to make a light sauce for chicken or fish. I also use it in fruit salads because it isn't as acid as wine vinegars. Try it sprinkled on cooked veggies. I've even had it with sautéed calf's liver garnished with whole raspberries. So don't say fruit-flavored vinegars don't have enough uses. *Makes 1 quart*

3 cups white, red or Chinese rice wine
    vinegar
1 cup raspberry liqueur (framboise)
2 or 3 drops red food coloring
    (optional)

Into a 1-quart bottle with a tight-fitting lid, pour the vinegar and liqueur. Add the food coloring, if desired. Store in a cool, dark place, where the vinegar will keep indefinitely.

Ginger Marmalade

Makes about 6 half-pint jars

*1½ cups fresh gingerroot (about 2 large
    knobs)*
10 cups cold water
4 cups + 1 tablespoon white sugar
*1 tablespoon finely shredded lemon peel
    (no white pith)*
½ cup lemon juice
3 ounces liquid pectin

Peel the gingerroot. Using a hand grater, grate only the outer third of the gingerroot into long shreds. Place the shredded ginger and 4 cups of the cold water in a large, heavy non-reactive pot and bring to a boil. Boil for 5 minutes. Drain the ginger and discard the water. Return the drained ginger to the pot and add the remaining 6 cups cold water. Add the sugar. Bring to a boil. Reduce the heat to very low and simmer, covered, for 1 hour. Uncover and stir in the shredded lemon peel. Cover again and allow to simmer for 30 minutes. Add the lemon juice. Raise the heat to high and bring to a rolling boil. Stir in the liquid pectin and boil for 1 minute. Remove the pot from the heat. Stir for a few minutes and let cool a little. Spoon into hot, dry, sterilized canning jars, leaving ¼-inch headspace in each jar. Seal according to manufacturer's directions.

Hot Chili Oil

I love hot and spicy foods. Making your own hot chili oil allows you the luxury of adding just a few drops of this molten fire to a dish, transforming it into another recipe altogether. For a taste surprise, try it in cold chicken salad or potato salad. Add a drop or two to your salad dressing, pasta sauce or scrambled or fried eggs. Experiment with this oil, using a very little at first, adding more the braver you become. *Makes 1 pint*

small dried hot chilis (the more you use, the hotter it gets)
1 pint light sesame oil

Wearing gloves, pack as many dried chilis as possible into a sterilized, heatproof bottle with a tight-fitting lid. Don't worry if some of the chilis break.

Heat the sesame oil until hot but not smoking. Allow to cool 10 minutes, then, using a funnel, pour it into the heatproof bottle, leaving ¼-inch headspace. When it is completely cool, close tightly and store in a cool, dark place for 2 weeks.

Strain the oil and rebottle in another sterilized bottle. You may put one or two whole chilis in the bottle for garnish. Seal tightly and store in a cool, dark place. Keeps indefinitely.

Five-Pepper Mélange

Five-pepper mélange is called for in several of the recipes in this book. Of course you may substitute freshly cracked black pepper, but it won't be nearly as tasty. I use this peppercorn mixture on everything from my breakfast eggs to my dinner salad, to meat, chicken, fish and even fruit. It's so much more fragrant than black pepper alone. If I had but one thing to say about this mixture, it would be to warn you that it can become habit-forming!

In a clear glass or Lucite peppermill, mix together equal amounts of the firtst five ingredients.

pink peppercorns
white peppercorns
black peppercorns
Szechuan peppercorns
dried green peppercorns and add 6 tiny
*   whole dried red peppers*

As a variation, I sometimes include a small amount of whole cloves.

Vanilla Extract

As a member of the American Orchid Society, I was pleased to visit a vanilla plantation in Tahiti. You see, the vanilla bean is the dried seed pod of the vanilla fragrans or vanilla plantifolia orchid. The flower of the orchid is undistinguished, but its flavorful gift of vanilla bean will endear it to me forever. You probably know most of its dessert uses: icings, cookies, cakes, custards, sauces, syrups and vanilla sugar. But the late actor Victor Buono once told me to add a split vanilla bean to the water in which I was cooking squid. It is an unbelievable combination. There are several varieties of vanilla bean available: Tahitian, Bourbon from Madagascar, and Mexican. You may substitute vodka for the cognac, but I prefer cognac or brandy. *Makes ½ cup*

½ cup cognac
4 vanilla beans, split in half lengthwise

Place the cognac and split vanilla beans in a tall, thin bottle. (Cut the beans to fit if you can't find a tall bottle.) Make sure that the beans are completely covered with the cognac. Seal the bottle and set the extract in a dark place to steep for 2 or 3 weeks. I like extract to contain the tiny vanilla seeds, but, if you prefer, you may strain it through cheesecloth that has been rinsed in water to remove any detergent residue and thoroughly wrung. Seal the bottle tightly again and store in a cool, dark place, where the extract will keep indefinitely.

Chèvre in Herbed Oil

Fresh, delicious *chèvre* made from goat's milk is now widely available. The French, of course, make a great *chèvre*, in many shapes and varieties. I also love the *chèvre* that is made in northern California. In the following recipe I use the log-shaped Montrachet, which slices into perfect rounds. *Chèvre* heats nicely and is great served warm in a salad or on a chicken breast, lightly browned under the broiler. *Makes 1 pint jar*

7 ounces extra virgin olive oil
½ cup chopped fresh chives, rosemary, dill or thyme, or a combination (or ¼ cup dried)
1 dried hot red chili pepper
2 garlic cloves, crushed and peeled
4 slices shallot
¼ teaspoon whole peppercorns (a combination of red, white, green and black)
1 tablespoon red wine vinegar
1 Montrachet "log," cut into ½-inch rounds
additional fresh herb sprigs for garnish
edible flowers (page 28) such as nasturtiums, pansies, bachelor's buttons, or calendula petals

Put half of the first 7 ingredients into a clean pint jar with a tight-fitting lid. Brush the *chèvre* slices with some of the remaining olive oil and press an herb sprig and flower petal of your choice into one side of each slice. Place the *chèvre* slices in the jar, herb sprig facing out, and pour in the remaining oil. (If the oil doesn't cover the cheese, add more until it does.) Carefully remove any air bubbles by inserting a narrow knife between the *chèvre* slices and the inside of the jar. Now add the remaining chopped herbs, chili pepper, garlic, shallot slices, peppercorns and vinegar. For color, top with additional edible flowers and herb sprigs. Store in the refrigerator; keeps for 1 month.

NOTE: Pansies lose their color in a couple of days. However, their beauty makes it more than worth-while if you either use the *chèvre* by the end of the third day or add them to the jar just before serving. All flower colors will alter slightly when steeped in oil.

Szechuan Vodka

Flavored vodkas are a delightful way to start a dinner party. It's especially fun to serve the bottle embedded in ice. Place the bottle inside a round or square container large enough to hold it with at least an inch of ice on all sides. Use boiled water that you have allowed to cool a little. That way your ice will be clear. Center the bottle and pour in the water to a depth of about 1½ inches. Freeze. When the water has frozen, add some decorations: flowers, leaves, herb sprigs or fresh red and green hot chili peppers. Pour in an inch or two of water and place the container in the freezer again. When this addition of water has frozen, add more decorations and water to complete your ice ring. When you are ready to remove the container from the ice, hold it under running water for a brief moment, until you can slide it free. As a courtesy, warn your guests about what they are about to experience when you serve this fiery drink. *Makes 1 quart*

4 cups 80 proof vodka or gin
¼ teaspoon pink peppercorns
¼ teaspoon Szechuan peppercorns
1 or 2 small hot dried red peppers
2 slices fresh gingerroot
1 slice lemon

Place all the ingredients in a 1-quart jar and seal tightly. Let the jar stand at room temperature for 6 to 10 hours. No longer! (The longer the peppers steep, the hotter the vodka.) Strain through a sieve lined with cheesecloth that has been rinsed in warm water to remove any detergent residue. If the vodka is clear, pour into bottles with tight-fitting caps, leaving ½-inch head-space. (If it is cloudy, strain through the cheesecloth again.) Seal tightly and freeze. Serve straight from the freezer.

Herb-Flavored Oils & Vinegars

Herb-flavored oils and vinegars are a boon to my cooking. To begin with, they enable me to add incredible flavors to almost all the dishes I make. Second, if anyone is on a salt-free or low-cholesterol diet, these oils and vinegars give a great flavor alternative. I always use pure, green, extra virgin olive oil, the best I can buy. But here it is not necessary. The pale, pure, golden olive oil has a lighter color and flavor. Light oils allow the hue and flavor of the herbs and spices to permeate them, imparting a color and taste bouquet that will adorn almost any dish, hot or cold. Any light, mild, polyunsaturated oil may be used. Flavored vinegars are similarly prepared, using a good red or white wine vinegar. Remember to warm, not heat, the oil or vinegar when using dried or fresh herbs to gently release their flavors.

**Herbed Vinegars and
Oils with Their
Ingredients**

Herb-Flavored Oil

Makes 1 quart

2 garlic cloves, peeled
1 shallot, peeled
1 thin slice lemon
1 quart pure virgin olive oil
3 sprigs each of any 3 herbs, such as tarragon, thyme, dill, rosemary or oregano
3 chives
3 each of white, black, pink and Szechuan peppercorns
1 or 2 small hot dried chili peppers
1 small bay leaf

On a bamboo skewer, thread the garlic cloves, shallot and the lemon slice. Slightly warm the oil. Do not allow it to get above 100°F or you will fry the herbs and seasonings. Pour half the oil into a liter-sized bottle. Put in the herb sprigs, bound and tied with the chives, the garlic-shallot skewer, the peppercorns, the hot chili peppers and the bay leaf. Pour in the remainder of the warm oil, leaving a ½-inch headspace, and seal the bottle. Put the bottle in a cool dark place for 10 to 14 days before using. By then the oil will have been infused with true gourmet goodness. If you have used fresh herbs, strain and repack the oil, retaining the skewered garlic if you like; otherwise, mold may form on the herbs that are exposed as the level of oil drops with use. If you wish, place a sprig or two of dried herbs in the bottle for easy identification. (When the garlic starts to turn an unattractive brown, in about 2 months, you can easily remove it from the skewer.)

Keeps well for up to a year, but I think you'll use it up a lot sooner.

Herb Vinegar #1

Try variations and combinations of herbs. I like thyme-lemon-shallot, dill-garlic-Szechuan peppercorn and chive-shallot-garlic. The combinations are as unlimited as your imagination. *Makes 1 quart*

1 quart red or white wine vinegar
10 fresh basil leaves
4 garlic cloves

Warm, but do not heat, the vinegar. Place the basil and garlic in a 1-quart bottle, and pour in the vinegar, leaving ¼-inch headspace. Seal tightly. If you find that the herbs become unattractively pale after being steeped in a cool, dark place for 2 weeks, strain the vinegar.

Herb Vinegar #2

1 quart white wine vinegar
4 sprigs fresh tarragon
2 garlic cloves
1 slice lemon

Proceed as for Herb Vinegar #1.

Spice Vinegar

I like to sprinkle this on Chinese food, salads, even fish and chips as a fun substitute for malt vinegar. Try it on chicken salad. It's also fabulous sprinkled on a plate of freshly boiled turnip or mustard greens, chard or kale.   *Makes 1 quart*

2 slices fresh gingerroot
1 cinnamon stick
1 tablespoon black peppercorns
1 tablespoon white peppercorns
1 tablespoon pink peppercorns
2 tablespoons yellow mustard seeds
1 tablespoon allspice
1 tablespoon ground mace
1 tablespoon whole cloves
1 quart white vinegar

Put the gingerroot and spices in a cheesecloth bag and tie well. Combine with the vinegar in a non-corrosive saucepan. Warm the vinegar to at least 100–125°F. Remove from heat and allow the vinegar to cool. Discard cheesecloth bag. When completely cool, pour into a hot, dry, sterilized 1-liter bottle, leaving ¼-inch headspace, and seal well.

Garlic Oil

I use this garlic oil in most of my salads and in any recipe that calls for garlic. The lionhearted may even enjoy scrambled eggs cooked in it! Thread a bamboo skewer or skewers with 10 to 20 peeled garlic cloves. Place the skewers in a sterilized canning jar or bottle, cover with olive oil, seal and store in a cool, dark place for a week to 10 days. When the garlic cloves start to turn brown, remove the skewers.

A great variation on this theme is lemon garlic oil. Simply alternate the garlic cloves with lemon slices on the skewer.

I encourage you to try variations of your own, including herbs. Two of my favorite combinations are lemon, dill and garlic; and lime, thyme and garlic.

Keeps well up to a year, if you remove the garlic.

Salads & Appetizers

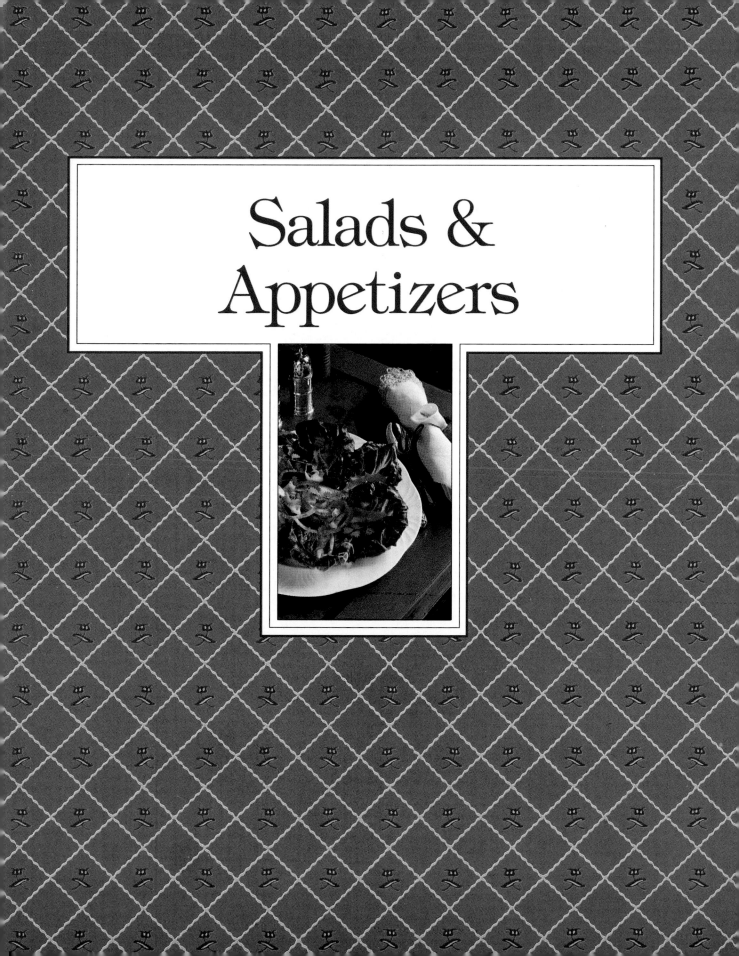

As an actress, I've learned that if the script doesn't grab you in the first fifteen minutes, it never will. To me the salad or appetizer is equivalent to those first fifteen minutes. It sets the tone for the entire dinner. Chosen carefully to complement the other recipes you have prepared, salad is often the only fresh, raw ingredient in our diets. Loaded with nutrients and dressed up or down with light or heavy dressings, they add balance to our meals. To me, "salad" doesn't have to mean lettuce. In this chapter I offer a few surprises such as vegetables, fruits, cheeses, rices, sushi rolls and edible flowers. Is that diverse enough for you?

In Europe, France particularly, salad is served after the main course. Here in America we serve it before the main course. I think we do it the correct way, because salad gets our digestive juices working and enables us to better digest our meal. All of us at one time or another have had a big salad for lunch or dinner and, what's more, we liked it. It's only fitting that the greatest agriculture-producing nation in the world should have its people enjoying salad on a daily basis.

Wilted Bibb Lettuce or Spinach Salad

Scandia restaurant in West Hollywood serves a wilted Bibb lettuce salad that I love. The dressing is prepared at the table in a chafing dish and tossed in a large wooden bowl. The dressing goes perfectly with spinach and Boston and butter lettuce as well as Bibb lettuce. I've watched the salad being prepared at my table for so many years now that I didn't even have to ask how it was made. *Serves 6–8*

10 slices sugar-cured bacon
1½ cups red wine vinegar
¼ cup bacon fat
½ cup olive oil
¼ cup chopped fresh chives
¼ cup chopped small green scallions
½ cup sugar
1 pound Bibb lettuce or spinach,
    washed and dried

Cook bacon thoroughly but do not allow to crisp. Drain on paper towels and chop into small pieces. Place vinegar, bacon fat, olive oil and chives in a saucepan. Bring to a boil, add scallions and sugar, and return to a boil. Add bacon and pour over the lettuce or spinach. Toss well and serve at once.

24 ☙ THE JILL ST. JOHN COOKBOOK

Orange & Onion Salad

~~~~~~

In the dead of winter it can be difficult to find a fresh and colorful salad. Thanks to Florida and California, oranges are always at hand. And onions—well, we can always find them. My orange and onion salad is one of those dishes that nobody wants to try, but once cajoled into it, most people ask for more. Try it! *Serves 4–6*

~~~~~~

VINAIGRETTE

½ cup red wine vinegar or Herb Vinegar (pages 18, 19)
1 cup olive oil or Garlic Oil (page 19)
¼ teaspoon salt
½ teaspoon Five-Pepper Mélange (page 10) or black pepper
1 teaspoon chopped fresh chives
1 teaspoon finely chopped tomato
1 teaspoon finely chopped onion
1 teaspoon finely chopped red pepper
1 teaspoon finely chopped Italian flat-leaf parsley
1 garlic clove, minced
¼ teaspoon sugar

3 seedless oranges, peeled (white pith removed)
2 mild white or red onions

Prepare the vinaigrette: Mix ingredients together in a bowl and set aside.

Slice the oranges and onions thinly, and lay them in alternating layers in a shallow glass or other non-reactive pan. Pour the dressing over the slices, cover and marinate in the refrigerator, turning the slices a couple of times, for 4 to 6 hours. Turn the onions gently so as not to break up the slices. Garnish with an additional sprinkling of pepper mélange, if desired.

Arugula, Radicchio, Endive & Ginger Salad

Salads are terribly important, nutritionally speaking. They balance our meals. The last few years have seen the easy availability of several formerly rare "greens" such as radicchio, arugula and Belgian endive. I encourage you to include these in your salads. Once their novelty wears off, you will come to think of them as staples. *Serves 8*

1 pound of any combination of the following: arugula, watercress, radicchio, or Belgian endive, torn into bite-sized pieces

1 large or 2 small red or Maui onions

2 teaspoons dried red chili peppers, crushed

1-inch piece fresh gingerroot, peeled and grated

2 tablespoons light soy sauce

3 tablespoons flavorless sesame or other light oil

1 teaspoon brown sugar

pinch salt

sprigs of salad burnet or other herbs for garnish (optional)

Wash and dry the greens and thinly slice the onions. Place in a large salad bowl.

In a small deep-sided sauté pan, combine the remaining ingredients and place over medium heat. When hot but not boiling, pour the dressing over the bowl of greens and toss very quickly. Garnish with salad burnet if desired, and serve at once.

Edible Flower Salad

Doug and Janelle's Garden in El Jebel, Colorado, introduced me to the delights of edible flowers. Janelle grows all of the edible flowers, herbs and flowering herbs that appear in this book, without pesticides or chemicals. Instead of telling you which flowers are inedible, I'm simply going to concentrate on some we can safely enjoy, such as pansies, nasturtiums, daisies, violas, violets, calendulas, gladioli, hollyhocks and bachelor's buttons.

This is my favorite party salad. Everyone ooohs and ahhhs when it is presented. And when they taste it, they all say they never thought they would really eat flowers and like them.

---

oakleaf lettuce
red oakleaf lettuce
green ice lettuce
baby beet greens
French sorrel
salad burnet
bachelor's button
nasturtium
gladiola petals
pansies
yellow plum tomatoes
baby red chard
calendula petals

Wash the greens and flower petals gently and dry in a salad spinner. Or use my favorite device—a clean pillowcase: Drain them in a colander and plop the whole lot into the pillowcase. Grab the open end of the case and swing it to release most of the water (somewhere you won't mind the water splattering!). You may store the pillowcase in the refrigerator until dinner time; it can easily be molded to fit any available space, and it will keep the salad crisp.

Toss with Herbed Vinaigrette Dressing (below) and serve at once.

Herbed Vinaigrette Dressing

½ cup cider vinegar

½ teaspoon salt

¼ teaspoon garlic salt

¼ teaspoon black pepper

1 cup olive oil

1 teaspoon finely chopped fresh chives

1 teaspoon finely chopped fresh thyme or dill

1 teaspoon finely chopped fresh Italian flat-leaf parsley

Vigorously mix ingredients together. Serve on Edible Flower Salad or other salads.

Edible Flower & Vegetable Sushi Rolls

Janelle is the only person I know who makes edible flower and vegetable sushi rolls. She has graciously agreed to share her method.

Sushi rolls, once you learn how to form them, are a quick and easy hors d'oeuvre. On a summer's evening, a tray of edible flower sushi rolls looks pretty, has a light touch and adds a very special something.

When packing a picnic hamper, I like to serve vegetable sushi rolls in place of salad. They travel well, take up less room, and add a touch of exotica to the meal. Vary the fillings according to what's in season and whether you intend to serve them as a salad, hors d'oeuvre, or cold side dish.

I'm working on other combinations, such as avocado and prosciutto, and pear and bacon. Invent your own combinations. *Makes 8 rolls*

FOR THE SUSHI RICE

4 cups rice (preferably short grain)
4 cups water
½ cup Sunomono rice wine vinegar
4 teaspoons white sugar
1½ teaspoons salt

Under cold running water, rinse the rice until the water runs clear. Drain completely. Put the rinsed rice in a large pot, add the 4 cups cold water and let the rice stand for 30 minutes. Put the pot over high heat and bring to a rapid boil. Boil for 1 minute. Cover pot and lower heat to a simmer. After 20 minutes, remove pot from heat and let stand, still covered, for 10 minutes. (Don't uncover the pot during this time.) Transfer the rice to a large bowl. (For best results, refrigerate the bowl first for 30 minutes.)

In a small bowl, mix the rice wine vinegar with the sugar and salt, stirring to dissolve completely. Sprinkle this mixture over the rice and toss very gently with a fork. Don't worry if the rice becomes sticky.

FORMING THE SUSHI ROLLS

bamboo mat (sushi sudare)
sushi rice (above)
8 sheets roasted seaweed (sushi nori)

FILLING INGREDIENTS

giant red mustard leaves
purple shiso
chives
*eggs, scrambled hard, cooled, and cut
    into strips*

FLOWERS

hollyhocks
calendulas
gladioli
daisies

*VEGETABLES (IN SMALL PIECES OR
JULIENNE STRIPS)*

carrots
small green beans (haricots verts)
turnips
roasted or raw peppers
zucchini
snowpeas
peeled, seeded and drained tomatoes
white radishes
raw peas
raw corn kernels
avocados
cucumbers
basil leaves
chives
celery
fennel
asparagus
nuts
scrambled egg strips

Place the bamboo mat on a flat surface. With your fingers, spread ⅔
cup of the sushi rice in an even layer
over two-thirds of the seaweed. (If
your fingers are slightly dampened it
will be easier to spread the rice.)
Turn the mat so that the uncovered
portion of the nori is away from you.
Place the filling ingredients in a row
across the portion of the rice nearest
you. (See Figure 1.)

Roll up the sushi, starting with
the end nearest you (the end with
the filling). Lightly roll away from
yourself. With your fingers, press
down slightly, every quarter turn.
You may want to rewrap the sushi
roll with the bamboo mat, pressing
slightly with your hands. (See Figure 2.)

Cut the sushi roll into four or
more pieces with a sharp knife. Dip
the knife in hot water before each
cut. Serve on a plate or tray.

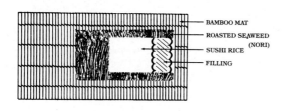

BAMBOO MAT
ROASTED SEAWEED
(NORI)
SUSHI RICE
FILLING

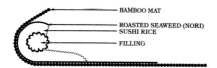

BAMBOO MAT
ROASTED SEAWEED (NORI)
SUSHI RICE
FILLING

Spicy Tomato & Onion Salad

Never store tomatoes in the fridge. Put them on a bright windowsill, where the rays of the sun will render them sweeter. *Serves 4*

2 large ripe beefsteak tomatoes
1 large white onion
1 teaspoon freshly grated gingerroot
½ large red bell pepper, thinly sliced
½ small jalapeño pepper, seeded and finely chopped
juice of 1 lemon

Peel, seed and coarsely chop the tomatoes. Thinly slice the onion and break into rings. Put the tomatoes and onions in a glass bowl.

In a smaller bowl, combine the grated gingerroot, red pepper slices, chopped jalapeño and lemon juice. Pour this mixture over the tomatoes and onion. Mix well and serve.

Chèvre Caprese

This dish, which originated in Capri, is traditionally made with sliced buffalo mozzarella. I like to substitute *chèvre* that I have put up in herbed olive oil. *Serves 4*

*12 thin slices Chèvre in Herbed Oil
    (page 18)*
12 slices ripe tomato
12 large fresh basil leaves
*freshly ground Five-Pepper
    Mélange (page 10) or black pepper*

Alternate three slices each of *chèvre* and tomato and three basil leaves on each plate. Drizzle with the herbed oil from the *chèvre* jar and sprinkle with the freshly ground Five-Pepper Mélange or black pepper.

Three-Rice Salad

~~~~~~

This is a great buffet dish for any time of the year. It will stand for a couple of hours without loss of flavor or texture. Do try to use the nasturtiums and calendulas; they really make this a stunning salad, one to be served at festive gatherings. *Serves 12*

~~~~~~

½ cup mayonnaise
¾ teaspoon dry mustard
3 garlic cloves, minced
1 tablespoon fresh lemon juice
1 cup (raw volume) wild rice, cooked and cooled
1 cup (raw volume) brown rice, cooked and cooled
1 cup (raw volume) long-grain white rice, cooked and cooled
½ cup chopped pecans or walnuts
2 oranges, peeled, seeded and chopped
2 apples, cored and chopped
1 tablespoon grated orange peel
3 green onions, sliced
10 to 12 edible nasturtium blossoms (optional)
petals of 4 calendula flowers (optional)

In a small bowl, mix together the mayonnaise, dry mustard, garlic and lemon juice. Set aside.

In a large bowl, combine the three rices, chopped nuts, oranges, apples, orange peel and sliced green onions. Add half of the mayonnaise mixture, half of the nasturtiums and all of the calendula petals, if used, and toss. Mix in the remaining mayonnaise and garnish with the remaining nasturtium flowers. Serve at room temperature.

Papaya & Avocado Salad

You can tell by this recipe that I was born in California. I attribute my good health in part to the fresh California fruits and vegetables on which I was raised. We had a huge avocado tree, and papayas were available in all the markets. Now that I live in Colorado, I'm forced to buy those grim, underripe avocados and green papayas and take them home for the "treatment," which consists of placing the avocados in a closed brown paper bag for three to six days to ripen. The papayas sit on a sunny windowsill and are turned over once or twice a day for three or four days or until they are fully ripened. At this point they are ripe enough to remind me of my childhood.
Serves 2

1 head romaine lettuce
1 ripe papaya
1 large or 2 small avocado(s)
¼ cup fresh lime juice
½ cup olive oil
*salt and freshly ground black pepper to
    taste*

Wash and dry the romaine, then tear it into large pieces. Peel and slice the papaya and avocado. Place the romaine, papaya and avocado in a salad bowl.

Mix together the lime juice, olive oil, salt and pepper to taste, pour over the salad.

This dressing also works well drizzled over avocado chunks mounded in the cavities of seeded papaya halves.

Limestone Lettuce with Lemon Cream Dressing

Lemon and cream—won't it curdle? It won't if you don't beat it. *Serves 4–6*

4 or 5 heads limestone lettuce
5 ounces whipping cream
1 ounce fresh lemon juice
salt and freshly ground pepper to taste

Wash and dry the lettuce and separate the leaves. Place them in a salad bowl.

Mix together the cream and lemon juice well, but *do not beat.* Add salt and pepper to taste. Just before serving, pour the dressing over the lettuce and toss well. Serve at once.

Soups

To me soup is the most basic, satisfying and diverse of all preparations. By the time primitive man had discovered fire and had developed crude implements to prepare foods, soup must have been born. A diet of spit-roasted meat had to be supplemented with greens, nuts and berries. Adding some water to that mess, cooked in a hollowed-out stone set over the fire, they must have created a sort of "caveman chowder." I don't think it would've tasted very good, but it was hot and it was filling. It warmed and soothed. Of course we demand those same qualities from our soups today, with the addition of great flavor.

No one dish has the versatility of soup; from the very refined, clarified consommés or shellfish bisques to the one-dish meals such as *pot-au-feu* or chicken in the pot, or even my favorite, *bouillabaisse*. Most soups have the same beginnings as the soup stock that you made from the bones and carcass of the type of stock you had in mind. Flavored with vegetables and herbs, your reduced stock is your ticket to hog heaven. You can then prepare crèmes, purées, potages, bisques and so on; in other words, soup of any kind. You might add to your finished soup: rice, tiny pasta, dumplings, matzoh balls, beaten or poached eggs, wontons, kreplachs, cream, sherry, ad infinitum.

We have all heard that chicken soup is Jewish penicillin. There have recently been scientific studies supporting its restorative properties. I believe its curative value comes from the aromatic steam that opens up a stuffed-up head and the delicious broth warming, soothing and nourishing us. Soup is easy to digest. Its liquid along with meats and vegetables are literally just what the doctor ordered. Chicken soup isn't the only ethnic penicillin. The Italians have minestrone and the Chinese have bird's nest soup as their respective penicillins. Now I wonder what the Mexicans use? or the Indians? Hmmm.

Cranberry-Beet Soup and Herbed French Bread

Carrot Soup with Thyme

Don't feel limited to carrots here. This basic recipe works well with broccoli, cauliflower, peas, beans and so on. Play with it. One night I tried parsnips, with a little freshly grated nutmeg for garnish. *Serves 4*

2 cups finely chopped onions
4 tablespoons unsalted butter
12 small sweet carrots (about 2 pounds)
4 cups chicken stock (homemade if possible, unsalted if canned)
¼ cup chopped fresh thyme, leaves only
salt and freshly ground pepper to taste
fresh thyme sprigs for garnish

Melt the butter in a large, deep-sided sauté pan. Add the onions and cook, covered, over low heat until soft, 20 to 25 minutes). Uncover, add carrots and chicken stock and bring to a boil. Lower heat and simmer for 30 minutes, or until carrots are soft. Strain and reserve stock. Purée carrots and onions in a blender or food processor. Add 1 cup of the stock to the purée and return to the pot. Slowly add more stock until the flavor and consistency seem right to you. Bring to a simmer. Add the chopped thyme leaves and salt and pepper to taste. Garnish with thyme sprigs.

This soup is also good served cold, with a dollop of sour cream or crème fraîche.

Potage Germiny (Cream of Sorrel Soup)

I've made three movies on location in the south of France. It was in the Negresco Hotel in Nice that I first tasted *potage germiny,* which I proceeded to order every day. This is my version of that classic. *Serves 6*

½ pound sorrel
2 tablespoons finely shredded carrot
6 cups chicken stock (homemade if possible, unsalted if canned)
2 egg yolks
¾ cup heavy cream
5 tablespoons unsalted butter, cut into small pieces
finely ground salt and ground white pepper to taste
chopped fresh chervil for garnish

Wash the sorrel well and remove the thick stems. Stack 10 or 12 leaves at a time, fold them over and shred finely with a knife. Repeat until all the sorrel has been shredded.

Fill a large, heavy saucepan with water to a depth of ⅛ inch. Bring the water to a boil and add the shredded sorrel and carrot, a large handful at a time, stirring until all the sorrel is just wilted. Lower heat, cover, and allow to simmer for 8 to 10 minutes, stirring occasionally to prevent sticking. Remove from heat and pour into a colander to drain.

In a medium stockpot, bring the chicken stock to a boil. Add the drained sorrel and carrot mixture. In a bowl, beat together the egg yolks and cream. Gradually stir 1 cup of the hot stock into the egg yolk-cream mixture and pour the mixture back into the pot. (This will prevent curdling.) Do not allow the soup to boil.

Remove the pot from the heat and stir in the cut-up butter. Season with salt and white pepper to taste. Garnish with chopped fresh chervil.

Potage Germiny and Three-Cheese Bread

Clear Mushroom Soup

One day I found too many mushrooms in the fridge, and this is the result. *Serves 6*

1¼ pounds mushrooms
*2 quarts chicken stock (homemade if
    possible, unsalted if canned)*
4 celery stalks, with leaves
½ large white or yellow onion
3 black peppercorns
salt to taste
1 tablespoon very finely chopped parsley

Reserve ¼ pound of the best-looking, most uniform mushrooms and slice the rest.

In a large pot, bring the stock, celery and onion to a boil. And the sliced mushrooms and return to the boil. Add the peppercorns and reduce the heat to a simmer. Allow to simmer gently for 2½ hours, or until the liquid is reduced by half.

Strain the soup and discard the mushrooms. Return the liquid to the pot, slice the remaining ¼ pound mushrooms and add to the pot. Simmer over medium heat for 10 minutes. Add salt to taste and the finely chopped parsley. Serve at once.

Cranberry-Beet Soup

Serves 6

¾ cup chopped shallots
1 tablespoon unsalted butter
a 1-pound can beets
3 cups chicken stock (homemade if
*   possible, unsalted if canned)*
1 pound raw cranberries, picked over
3 or 4 teaspoons fresh lemon juice
¼ cup sherry or Madeira
salt and freshly ground pepper to taste
sour cream for garnish
fresh dill sprigs for garnish

Sauté the chopped shallots in the butter over low heat, until soft and transparent. Do not brown.

Place the beets with their juice in a blender or in a food processor fitted with the steel blade. Add the cooked shallots and blend or process until puréed. Transfer the mixture to a glass bowl. (Do not wash out the work bowl.)

Place the chicken stock and cranberries in a large pot and bring to a simmer. Simmer over medium heat until the cranberries split, about 5 minutes. Remove from heat and allow to cool slightly. Place the chicken stock-cranberry mixture in the work bowl and purée. Strain the purée through a metal sieve and force the solids through with the back of a spoon. Combine the cranberry and beet purées and add lemon juice to taste, the sherry or Madeira, and salt and pepper to taste.

Serve hot or cold, each serving garnished with a dollop of sour cream and a dill sprig.

Sea Scallop Chowder

Winter's cold, snowy days demand hot soup. This sea scallop chowder is a great filler-upper and warmer-upper. Do insist that your fish merchant include the scallop's coral roe. A lot of folks throw it away, unaware of its delicate flavor and great texture. Besides, it's pretty. *Serves 4–6*

1 pound shucked sea scallops with their coral roe
3 tablespoons unsalted butter
1 large white onion, chopped
1 cup chopped celery
⅓ cup clam juice
¼ teaspoon sugar
1 tablespoon finely chopped thyme
1 tablespoon finely chopped fresh rosemary
½ teaspoon salt
½ teaspoon white pepper
3 cups half-and-half
sweet paprika for garnish
chopped parsley for garnish

Cut the scallops and roe into bite-sized pieces. Melt the butter in a large, deep-sided sauté pan, add the chopped onion and celery and cook over medium-low heat until they are soft and transparent. Do not brown. Add the scallops and roe, the clam juice and the sugar. Reduce heat to low and stir in the thyme, rosemary, salt and pepper. Add the half-and-half and heat until hot. Do not allow to boil.

Garnish with a pinch of the paprika and chopped parsley.

Cream of Cucumber Soup

When served cold, this is a perfect summer soup. I always seem to accompany it with its natural mate—cold poached salmon. It also goes beautifully with swordfish, halibut, whitefish and, of course, hot or cold chicken. Serve it hot, though, with beef or lamb. *Serves 8*

3 cups coarsely chopped cucumber plus additional finely chopped for garnish

1½ cups chicken stock (homemade if possible, unsalted if canned)

1½ cups half-and-half

½ cup chopped chives

½ cup chopped celery leaves

6 sprigs parsley

3 tablespoons unsalted butter, softened

3 tablespoons all-purpose flour

salt and white pepper to taste

finely chopped dill for garnish (optional)

Place all the ingredients except the salt and pepper in a blender or food processor and purée until smooth. Transfer to a saucepan and heat slowly until it reaches a boil. Remove from heat and season with salt and white pepper to taste.

Serve hot, garnished with finely chopped dill, or cold, garnished with finely chopped cucumber and dill.

Ginger Squash Soup

Serves 6

2 pounds acorn or butternut squash
3 tablespoons unsalted butter or
    margarine
2 large onions, sliced
2 tart green apples, peeled, cored and
    chopped, Granny Smith or Pippin
3 celery stalks, chopped
2 garlic cloves, minced
6 slices fresh gingerroot
3 cups chicken stock (homemade if
    possible, unsalted if canned)
1 cup cream (heavy or light)
3 tablespoons dry sherry
1½ tablespoons fresh lime juice

Peel the squash and cut it into ½-inch cubes. (It may be easier to peel if you cut it in half and bake it on a baking sheet, cut side down, in a preheated 375°F oven for 15 to 20 minutes.)

Melt the butter in a large pot. Add the onions, apples and celery and cook over medium heat until the onions are translucent. Do not brown. Add the minced garlic, squash, ginger and chicken stock. When the stock comes to a boil, lower the heat and allow to simmer until the squash is tender, about 20 minutes.

Purée the soup in a food processor or blender. Warm the cream and stir it in. Stir in the sherry and lime juice. Serve hot.

Clam Broth

I love to serve clam broth for Christmas dinner. Do use bottled spring water (non-carbonated) for all your soups and even coffee when possible, because most city water systems serve up water that contains too many chemicals and tastes disgusting.

The first year I bought my "ranchette" in Aspen, the entire neighborhood (all sixteen homes) ran out of water. It seems that our water table was very low and the spring that feeds our houses had dried up temporarily. (We irrigate our fields from another water source.) After two days of nothing but dust coming out of the taps and no working toilets, I decided to drill my own well. I called our local "water witch," who found a water source near the house. The drillers dug on the "witched" spot for a couple of days and finally struck oil! I was terribly upset—you see, I didn't need oil, I needed water. I made them keep drilling and at 250 feet they reached a pool of pure, sweet water. Was I relieved! That was fifteen years ago. The spring has never dried up again, but I wouldn't trade my pure, sweet well water for anything—including oil. *Serves 12*

75 to 80 clams (cherrystones are best)
3 quarts water
4 celery stalks, with leaves
salt to taste (optional)
Whipped Horseradish Cream (below)

Scrub the clams and shuck them over a bowl to catch the juices. (Or try to con your fish merchant into doing this for you.)

Remove clams from juice and chop them coarsely. Place the clams with their juice and the spring water in a large saucepan and add the celery. Bring to a boil and simmer for 25 minutes over medium heat. Strain the broth through a kitchen towel that has been rinsed in warm water several times to remove any soap or detergent residue.

Add salt only if necessary. Ladle into individual bowls or cups and top with a scant teaspoon of the horseradish cream.

Whipped Horseradish Cream

Makes 2 cups

½ pint whipping cream
½–1 teaspoon finely grated fresh horseradish (see Note)

Whip the cream until almost stiff. Add ½ teaspoon horseradish or to taste and beat until stiff. (Don't overbeat or the cream will turn to butter.)

NOTE: Horseradish gives off a very potent fume, so don't stand directly over it when grating. I grate it in my food processor and am very careful not to get the vapors in my eyes and nose.

Clam Chowder

Serves 6

24 large clams (I use cherrystones.)
8 strips bacon
3 tablespoons unsalted butter
2 large onions, chopped
2 Idaho potatoes, cut into ½-inch cubes
1 cup fresh corn kernels (2 to 3 ears)
2 cups fresh or bottled clam juice
½ cup heavy cream or half-and-half
salt and freshly ground pepper to taste
chopped chives for garnish
paprika for garnish

Shuck the clams over a bowl to catch their juices. Cut them into small pieces and reserve both clams and juice.

Dice the bacon and cook it in a large sauté pan until almost crisp. Drain well between thicknesses of paper towels. Pour off all the bacon grease and add the butter. Add the onions and sauté over medium heat until soft and transparent. Add the potatoes and continue to sauté for 5 to 6 minutes, stirring. Add the corn kernels, stir, and cook over medium-low heat until potatoes and corn are tender.

Add the chopped clams, their juices and the fresh or bottled clam juice. Simmer 2 to 3 minutes, until the clams are cooked. (If you over-cook them the clams will be tough.) Add the cream and heat, but do not boil. Season with salt and pepper to taste, and garnish each serving with chopped chives and a dusting of paprika.

Fish & Seafood

What is it about men? Most men won't eat fish. Did their mothers overcook it into a tough, flavorless lump? If you start children out with "just cooked" tender and flavorful fish, they will love it. And they will think that their playmates who don't eat fish are weird—which is the way *I* feel about anyone who won't eat fish.

To me, fish is the best food value of all, high in protein, low in fat, offering great flavor and unlimited methods of preparation. Could you ask for more? Ounce for ounce, its food and flavor value is excellent.

There is one rule that applies to all fish and seafood: *Don't overcook.* If you do, tenderness, texture and taste are lost. I love fish cooked just to the point of doneness, when the flesh in the very center is no longer translucent. If my serving dish is hot, and the fish finishes cooking on the way to the table, I'm happy. The rule of thumb is: 10 minutes cooking time for each 1-inch thickness of fish.

Chinese Steamed Fish

This is my favorite fish recipe. Almost fat- and salt-free, it has a clean, crisp taste, a tender texture and, for me, the added bonus of ginger. *Serves 4–6*

*a 2- to 3-pound whole fish or 2 to 3
    pounds fish filets, such as rock cod,
    sea bass, orange roughy, perch, sole
    or halibut*
*2–3 inch piece fresh gingerroot, cut into
    thin julienne*
5 scallions, cut into thin julienne
*12 sprigs cilantro (also known as
    Chinese parsley or coriander)*
½ teaspoon soy sauce
*2 teaspoons flavorless sesame oil (avail-
    able in health-food stores)*
6 tablespoons Chinese rice wine vinegar

Clean and rinse fish; pat dry. Place it in a deep plate that will fit inside a steamer or a large frying pan with cover. If using a whole fish, put one half the ginger, scallions and cilantro into the fish cavity and strew the rest on top. If you are using filets, place half the ginger and scallions on the plate, cover with the filets and strew the remaining ginger and scallions on top. Sprinkle with the soy sauce, sesame oil and rice wine vinegar. Allow to marinate at room temperature, covered, for 20 to 30 minutes.

Pour an inch or two of water into the bottom of the steamer. (If you don't have a steamer, use a large frying pan. Simply add an inch or two of water, invert an old metal pie plate in it, cover, and bring the water to a boil. Uncover carefully, lifting the lid away from your face, and position the plate of fish on top of the inverted pie plate.) When the water starts to boil, put in the plate of fish. Cover and steam over high heat until done, about 20 minutes. Serve the fish with the juices that have accumulated in the plate.

Bouillabaisse

From *bouillabaisse* to *zuppa di pesce* to *cioppino*, there is a common theme: fish stew, or soup if you prefer, prepared with chunks of fish and shellfish in a rich fish stock, enhanced with saffron. In my version, I include a small amount of fennel, which I think adds a fragrance that is distinctive but not overpowering.

The tiger prawns called for in this recipe are the huge ones that come from Thailand. They can weigh up to six or eight ounces each. Any type of prawn or very large shrimp will do, so use whatever you find fresh at your fish market.
Serves 12

1 pound or more of fish heads, tails, bones, and so on
2 quarts water
2 onions, quartered
3 celery stalks
1 small fennel bulb, halved (or half a large bulb), feathery leaves reserved
1 large bay leaf
2 teaspoons salt
2 black peppercorns
1 live lobster, about 1½ pounds
12 large tiger prawns

3 pounds medium raw shrimp in their shells
3 pounds fish filets (bass, halibut, swordfish, red snapper, whitefish, salmon, orange roughy), cut into chunks
1 pound squid, cleaned
12 sea scallops
2 tablespoons finely chopped parsley
1 tablespoon chopped fresh thyme, or 1 teaspoon dried
5 garlic cloves
⅓ cup extra virgin olive oil

3 tomatoes, peeled, seeded and roughly
  chopped
⅓ cup dry white wine
¼ teaspoon saffron threads
salt and pepper to taste
12 hard-shelled clams
12 mussels

Place the water in a large stockpot and add the fish heads, tails and bones, the quartered onions, celery, fennel bulb, bay leaf, salt and peppercorns. Bring to a boil and immediately plunge the live lobster into the stock. Boil for 5 minutes, then remove the lobster, drain and let cool.

While the lobster is cooling, plunge the tiger prawns into the boiling stock. Add the shrimp. Boil for 2 minutes, then lower the heat to a simmer, and remove the shrimp and prawns with a slotted spoon. Let cool.

Shell the lobster, cover and reserve the meat. Shell and devein the prawns and shrimp, and cover them too. Return all the shells to the stock and allow to simmer gently for 20 to 25 minutes—no longer, or the fish bones will make the stock bitter.

While the stock is simmering, cut the lobster, the assorted fish filets and the squid into 1½-inch chunks. Place them in a large bowl, cover and refrigerate.

When the stock has simmered gently for 20 to 25 minutes, remove from the heat. Strain through a large metal strainer lined with a cheesecloth that has been rinsed several times to remove any detergent residue. Set aside.

Finely chop 1 tablespoon of the leafy green fennel leaves and mix with the parsley and thyme. Mince the garlic and add it to the chopped herbs. Pour the olive oil into a large, deep-sided sauté pan and place over medium heat. Add the garlic-herb mixture and stir for a moment. Stirring constantly, add the chunks of fish and shellfish and cook, stirring, for 5 minutes. Pour in the strained fish stock and add the tomatoes, white wine, saffron, and salt and pepper to taste. Bring to a boil, then reduce heat to a simmer.

Scrub the clams and mussels well and add them to the *bouillabaisse*. Cover and simmer about 10 to 15 minutes, until the shells open. (Discard any shells that don't open.)

Serve the traditional way, in wide shallow soup bowls poured over a thick slice of freshly baked French bread sautéed in garlic oil.

Salmon & Tomatoes

This is one of those recipes that came of necessity. In other words, I thought I had some fresh dill and lemons at home when I purchased the salmon. But *noooo*. So I raided my orchid house, which has a shelf for fresh herbs. The only thing that looked good that day was the basil. Basil and salmon? Basil and salmon and cherry tomatoes? Yeah!
Serves 2

1 garlic clove, minced
juice of ½ lemon
3 tablespoons unsalted butter (or half butter, half olive oil)
¼ cup chopped fresh basil
12 cherry tomatoes
two 1-inch-thick salmon steaks or filets (about 8 ounces each)

Preheat broiler.

In a blender or food processor fitted with the steel blade, blend together the garlic, lemon juice and butter. Add the basil and process until the basil is chopped finely and the mixture is smooth. Add the tomatoes and process—on, off, on, off—until they are coarsely chopped.

Place the salmon in a baking pan and spread with half the tomato mixture. Broil about 3 inches from the flame, for 5 minutes. Turn the fish, cover with the remaining sauce, and broil 5 more minutes, or until done.

Serve with the pan juices poured over the salmon.

Salmon or Swordfish au Poivre

Serves 2

¼ teaspoon white peppercorns

¼ teaspoon black peppercorns

¼ teaspoon pink peppercorns

¼ teaspoon Szechuan peppercorns or 1 teaspoon Five-Pepper Mélange (page 10)

olive oil

two 1-inch-thick salmon or swordfish steaks (about 8 ounces each)

1 tablespoon flavored vinegar (such as shallot, sherry or garlic)

Coarsely grind the peppercorns or Five-Pepper Mélange. Pour just enough olive oil into a medium deep-sided sauté pan to cover the bottom. Place over high heat and sprinkle the ground peppers evenly in the pan. When hot, add the fish steaks and sear quickly on both sides. Lower the heat and cover the steaks with a lid that is smaller than the pan. Cook 3 to 4 minutes. Uncover and turn the steaks. Cover again and cook 4 to 5 minutes, or until done. Remove the cooked fish to a heated platter.

Raise the heat under the pan and stir the sauce. When it starts to get bubbly, add the flavored vinegar. Stir until the sharp vinegar smell has evaporated and the sauce has thickened slightly. Pour over the swordfish or salmon and serve at once.

Salmon or Swordfish au Poivre and Limestone Lettuce with Lemon Cream Dressing

Salmon & Seafood Boudins

Order sausage casings from your market or butcher. Soak them for 1 hour in vinegared water (about 1 cup vinegar to 2 quarts water). Rinse under running water to check for leaks. Discard any punctured casings. Soak again in fresh, cold water for 20 to 30 minutes. Drain, squeeze dry and fill as desired, leaving room for expansion during cooking. *Serves 4–6*

a 1-pound salmon filet
3 egg whites
1 egg yolk
¼ pound small bay shrimp, shelled
¼ pound king crab legs, shelled and cut into ¼-inch pieces
¼ cup pine nuts
4 tablespoons chopped fresh thyme
4 tablespoons chopped fresh chives
2 tablespoons chopped Italian flat-leaf parsley
salt and white pepper to taste
4–6 sausage casings
Mustard Dill Sauce (opposite)
dill sprigs for garnish

In the work bowl of a food processor fitted with the steel blade, process the salmon, egg whites and egg yolk to a smooth purée. Transfer to a large bowl and mix in the shrimp, crab, pine nuts, thyme, chives and parsley. Season with salt and white pepper to taste.

Fill the sausage casings with the mixture, using a pastry tube or sausage horn, and twist and tie the ends securely. Steam the sausages for 10 to 12 minutes. Slice and serve on individual plates, surrounded by the Mustard Dill Sauce. Garnish with dill sprigs. (I prefer to peel my *boudins* before carefully slicing but it is not necessary.)

Mustard Dill Sauce

Makes ²/₃ cup

*3 tablespoons Dijon or other sharp
    mustard*
¹/₂ cup good olive oil
2–3 tablespoons chopped fresh dill
2¹/₂ tablespoons white wine vinegar
1¹/₂ tablespoons white sugar
salt and freshly ground pepper to taste

With a rotary beater or whisk, blend all of the ingredients until you have a smooth sauce. Cover and refrigerate for 6 to 12 hours, to allow the flavors to develop.

Serve with salmon and seafood *boudins* or cold poached salmon or chicken.

Rocky Mountain Trout

My favorite fisherman and I love to fish the rivers of Colorado. We usually use dry flies, and we almost always catch and release. However, a brook trout the size of the one he is holding was destined for my cast iron skillet, so he brought it home. We adore spending our days in the middle of the Roaring Fork or Frying Pan rivers (we wear waders), absorbing the incredible beauty of the Rockies. I've also fished for yellowtail (which is great raw) in Baja and salmon in British Columbia. *Servings depend on quantity of fish*

2–3 eggs, beaten
fresh trout, gutted, cleaned and patted
*   dry*
equal amounts of cornmeal and white
*   flour*
salt and pepper
peanut oil

Pour the beaten eggs into a large shallow pan.

Dip the trout into the beaten eggs, turning to coat all sides. Mix together the cornmeal and flour and place in a separate pan or on a plate. Dip the fish into the cornmeal-flour mixture and coat well. Sprinkle with salt and pepper. Heat the peanut oil in a large heavy skillet, add the trout and fry until crusty, about 4 to 5 minutes on each side.

Abalone Cannelloni

Serves 6

6 abalone steaks, fresh or frozen (or 3
 pounds canned abalone)
7 tablespoons unsalted butter
flour for dredging
1 cup cooked and coarsely chopped
 shrimp
1 cup cooked and coarsely chopped
 lobster
1/4 cup grated cheddar cheese
1/4 cup ricotta or cream cheese
2 tablespoons chopped fresh chives
a 4-ounce jar pimientos, drained and
 chopped
1/8 teaspoon each dried oregano,
 rosemary, ground allspice, ground
 ginger, salt and pepper
3 tablespoons flour
2 1/4 cups milk, heated
3/4 teaspoon salt
1/8 teaspoon white pepper
1/4 cup champagne or dry white wine
1/2 cup mushrooms, lightly sautéed (or a
 4-ounce can button mushrooms,
 drained)

Preheat oven to 350°F.

Have your fish merchant slice the abalone steaks thin and pound them to a pulpy texture. Spread the steaks with 4 tablespoons of the butter, softened, and dredge them lightly in the flour.

Mix together the shrimp, lobster, cheeses, chives, pimientos and seasonings. Divide the filling evenly among the abalone steaks, spreading it evenly on the pieces, roll them up, and place them, seam side down, in a single layer in a buttered baking dish. (If using canned abalone, split them in half, pound them and sandwich the filling between the halves. Eliminate the butter and flour coating entirely.)

Melt the remaining 3 tablespoons butter in a saucepan over medium heat. Add the flour and whisk until smooth. Gradually add the milk, bring to a boil and cook, stirring constantly, until thickened. Add the salt, white pepper and champagne or wine and simmer 3 minutes. Remove from heat and stir in mushrooms. Pour the sauce over the abalone "cannelloni" and bake for 25 minutes, or until bubbling. Place under the broiler for a minute or two to brown the top lightly.

Ginger Lemon Shrimp

Here is yet another example of my continuing love affair with ginger. I'd put ginger in my eggs if I thought it would work. *Serves 4*

a 3-inch piece of fresh gingerroot
5 garlic cloves, minced
¼ teaspoon cayenne pepper
⅛ teaspoon white pepper
¾ cup fresh lemon juice
1 pound shelled and deveined raw shrimp
3 tablespoons peanut or corn oil
1 teaspoon Hot Chili Oil (page 9)
2 teaspoons black mustard seeds or poppy seeds
2 tablespoons chopped fresh chives for garnish

Peel the gingerroot and cut into small pieces. Place them in a food processor fitted with the steel knife and process until finely minced. Add the garlic, peppers and lemon juice, and process until blended. Place the shrimp in a large glass mixing bowl, add the lemon-ginger mixture, and toss until the shrimp are completely coated. Allow the shrimp to marinate, covered, in the refrigerator, turning them occasionally, for 1½ hours.

Scrape the marinade from the shrimp and place them in another bowl. Reserve the marinade. In a large, deep-sided sauté pan, heat the two oils over medium heat, until hot, but not smoking. Add the mustard or poppy seeds and sauté for 1 minute. Pour in the marinade and stir until thick. Do not allow it to change color. (If it starts to turn gold, take it off the heat.) Add the shrimp, stir and cook over medium heat for a couple of minutes until they are just cooked through.

Serve over steamed rice and garnish with the chopped chives.

Fiery Cajun Shrimp

I was first served Cajun shrimp at a dinner party in Aspen. I simply refused to leave until I was given the recipe, which comes from New Orleans. They are very rich, very *hot*, and very good!

These shrimp are messy but great fun and a real ice-breaker at a party. Serve with either hot towels or finger-bowls. (Hot towels are a lot less formal; fingerbowls seem too fancy for this Cajun delight.) If you have any sauce left over, which I doubt, refrigerate it, cov-ered, for four or five days or freeze it, covered, for up to six weeks. It's great on chicken, meat or fish. *Serves 10–12*

*5–6 pounds large raw shrimp in their
   shells*
½ pound unsalted butter, melted
½ pound margarine, melted
3–4 ounces Worcestershire sauce
*4 tablespoons freshly ground black pep-
   per*
1 teaspoon ground rosemary
juice of 2 lemons
2 teaspoons Tabasco sauce
2 teaspoons salt
3 garlic cloves, minced
2 lemons, sliced

Preheat oven to 400°F.

With a small, sharp pair of scissors, cut through the shells of the shrimp from top to tail. Do not cut the tails. Devein the shrimp but leave them in their shells.

In a bowl, mix together all the remaining ingredients except the lemon slices. Cover the bottom of a 13- × 9-inch glass baking dish with a little of this mixture. Arrange the shrimp and the lemon slices in layers in the dish, stopping about 1 inch from the top. Pour the remainder of the butter sauce over. Bake turning the shrimp once or twice, until they are cooked through, about 15 to 20 minutes.

Serve with hot French bread and an empty bowl for the shells. Your guests should open the shrimp shells with their fingers and dip the bread into the sauce.

Fish & Chips

Serves 4–6

2 pounds fresh white fish filets (cod,
     flounder, haddock), skinned and cut
     into 3-inch pieces
1 cup all-purpose flour
½ teaspoon salt
1 egg yolk, at room temperature
1 cup beer, at room temperature
2 pounds baking potatoes
vegetable oil for deep frying
2 egg whites, at room temperature
dash of salt
white cider or malt vinegar or Spice
     Vinegar (page 19)

Wash the filets and pat dry. Cover and set aside.

Combine the flour and salt in a large mixing bowl and make a well in the center. In a separate bowl, lightly beat the egg yolk, add the beer gradually, then pour the mixture into the well. Whisk the batter until just smooth, working from the center of the well to the outer edges of the bowl. Do not overwork. Set the batter aside to rest for 45 minutes to 1 hour. This resting period allows the gluten in the flour to relax and expand, producing a lighter batter that will coat the fish evenly.

Meanwhile, prepare the chips: Peel the potatoes, only if desired. (I don't peel mine, as the skins contain valuable potassium.) Slice them into ½-inch sticks. Rinse the potatoes and dry them thoroughly with a towel. (This is important, since beads of moisture may cause the hot oil in which they are fried to splatter and burn you.)

Preheat the oven to 250°F.

In a deep fat fryer or a deep, heavy pot fitted with a frying basket, heat about 4 inches of oil to 375°F. Deep fry the chips in small batches until golden and crisp, about 8 to 10 minutes. Drain on paper towels, transfer to a baking pan lined with paper towels, and keep warm in the oven.

Prepare the fish: In a clean, dry bowl, beat the egg whites until they form soft peaks. Gently fold the beaten egg whites into the egg batter until just blended.

Dip a few pieces of fish at a time into the batter. When thoroughly coated, put them carefully into the hot oil in which you fried the potatoes. (Check to see that it's still at

375°F.) Deep fry the fish, a few pieces at a time, about 5 to 10 minutes, until golden brown. Remove the filets as they brown, drain on paper towels, and transfer to a heated platter.

Mound the fish in the center and surround with the potatoes. If desired, serve the traditional British way, with a dash of salt and malt vinegar, or, less traditionally, with your own spice vinegar.

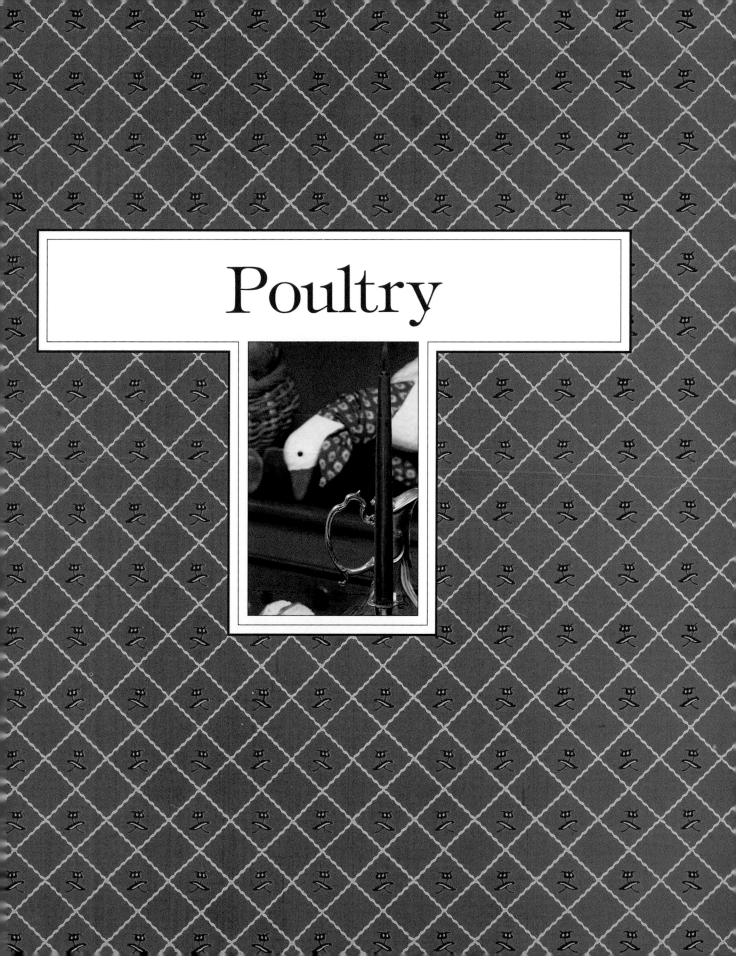

Poultry

High in protein, low in fat. The magic words, the magic food, you might say. Well, chicken can be, if you treat it properly. But you have to locate good chickens. A few more markets now sell free-range chickens that are tasty and good for us. But what about those of us who can't find these rare birds? Buy good-quality chicken, inquiring whether they were fed on hormones and antibiotics. If the answer is *yes,* try to find organically grown chickens elsewhere. A health food store can usually point you in the right direction. But whatever kind you purchase, always remove the skin. Chicken skin holds most of the fat and cholesterol, so throw it away. If you are served chicken with the skin on, trim it off. Except for goose and duck (and in this chapter, I'll tell you how to remove their fat) most other birds are fairly fat free. Turkey, pheasant, guinea hens, for example, are very low in fat. Fowl is delicious hot or cold. It takes or goes without sauces very well. What more do you want from a bird that is inexpensive and easy to get?

For the last three years we have kept chickens, for their fertile eggs, not for their meat. Since I feel I have a personal relationship with these birds, I can't bring myself to eat them. (Fortunately, the chickens at the market are total strangers.) However, I am not above threats. You see, occasionally, due to cold weather or other factors, the hens stop laying. I have been known to stand in front of the henhouse (we call it "Hotel de Coop") brandishing my favorite copper pan, yelling words like "coq au vin, chicken pot pie, chicken and peppers." Sounds crazy? The very next day always finds a few more eggs.

Roast Chicken with Lemon Honey Butter

Cinnamon Chicken

There is some debate as to whether the use of cinnamon with chicken, beef and lamb is a Mexican or Moroccan invention. All I know is that I like it. On its own, cinnamon is bitter. Sugar or honey must accompany it.

This dish may be served with my Lemon and Orange Rice (page 185) or my Puréed Rutabaga (page 174) and a green veggie. *Serves 3–4*

½ cup sherry
⅓ cup honey
2 teaspoons cinnamon
2 garlic cloves, crushed
salt and pepper to taste
2 tablespoons fresh lemon juice
1 small (3-pound) frying chicken, cut into serving pieces

Blend together the first 6 ingredients and pour over the chicken pieces. Allow the chicken to marinate, covered, for 6 hours or overnight, turning occasionally.

Preheat broiler and cook, about 3 inches from the heat, turning once, until done to your taste, 20 to 30 minutes. (The white meat will cook faster than the dark.)

Peachy Chicken

Paenonio, Colorado, grows great cherries, apricots and peaches. A lot of my friends in Aspen buy them in bulk and dry or preserve them. I bought a lot of peaches one day, only to discover I had lost my enthusiasm for canning. Hence, Peachy Chicken. *Serves 6*

two 2½- to 3-pound frying chickens, cut
*   into serving pieces*
salt and freshly ground white pepper
4 tablespoons unsalted butter
1 tablespoon olive oil
2 large white onions, finely chopped
3 cups chicken stock (homemade if pos-
*   sible, unsalted if canned)*
6 ripe peaches, peeled, pitted, sliced and
*   drizzled with lemon juice to prevent*
*   discoloring, with extra slices re-*
*   served for garnish.*
2 tablespoons warm peach brandy
1 teaspoon ground mace
¼ cup all-purpose flour

Remove any excess fat from the chicken pieces and sprinkle them lightly on all sides with a little salt and white pepper. In a large, deep-sided sauté pan, brown the chicken pieces in 3 tablespoons of the butter and the olive oil over medium-high heat. Remove pan from the heat with a spatula or slotted spoon, transfer the chicken pieces to a large range-proof casserole or deep-sided pan with a fitted lid. Return sauté pan to the heat and sauté the chopped onions in the butter and oil remaining in the pan until soft and light golden in color. Do not brown. Spoon the sautéed onions over the chicken pieces and pour in 1½ cups of the chicken stock. Do not wash the sauté pan.

Bring the chicken to a simmer, cover and cook over low heat for 25 minutes.

Melt the remaining tablespoon of butter in the sauté pan over high heat, add the peach slices, and brown very quickly, turning them with a spatula. Add the warm peach brandy. When the alcohol has evaporated, lower the heat to medium-low and sprinkle the peach slices with the mace and flour. Gently stir the peaches with a wooden spoon until the flour and mace are evenly distributed. Gradually stir in the remaining 1½ cups chicken stock. Allow to cool, stirring, until the sauce has thickened, about 10 to 15 minutes.

Uncover the casserole and pour the peach sauce over the chicken. Replace the cover and cook over low heat for 15 to 20 minutes. Remove cover. If the chicken still does not seem tender enough, continue to cook, uncovered, for 5 to 10 minutes more. Add salt and pepper to taste. Garnish with the remaining peach slices.

Ginger Fried Chicken

Serves 3–4

a 2½- to 3-pound frying chicken, cut
   into serving pieces
about 2 cups milk or buttermilk
1 cup all-purpose flour
2 tablespoons ground ginger
1 teaspoon garlic salt
1 teaspoon freshly ground white pepper
⅓ cup unsalted butter
⅔ cup light flavorless vegetable oil

Place the chicken snugly in a bowl or pot, add the milk or buttermilk to cover, and let soak for 10 minutes. Drain.

In a large paper bag, mix together the flour, ground ginger, garlic salt and white pepper. Put 2 or 3 pieces of chicken into the paper bag, roll the top of the bag to seal, and shake until the chicken pieces are coated. Repeat with the remaining chicken pieces.

Heat the butter and oil over medium heat in a large, deep-sided saucepan with a lid. Add the chicken pieces gradually, 1 or 2 at a time, and brown quickly on all sides. (Adding them to the pan too quickly will lower the temperature of the oil too much.) When the chicken pieces are browned on all sides, cover the pan and cook for 20 minutes over low heat. Remove the lid and cook, uncovered, for 20 to 25 minutes more, turning occasionally, until brown all over and cooked through.

Serve hot or cold.

Baked Garlic (with a Little Chicken)

Serves 6

two 2½- to 3-pound frying chickens, cut into serving pieces
1 lemon, halved
½ cup olive oil
4 tablespoons dry white wine
3 sprigs fresh thyme, chopped
1 sprig rosemary, chopped
1 small sprig dill, chopped
1 celery stalk with leaves, chopped
2 fennel bulbs with green feathery leaves, chopped
3 sprigs Italian flat leaf parsley, chopped
salt and freshly ground black pepper to taste
4 heads garlic, separated into cloves but unpeeled
1 small bay leaf

Preheat oven to 325°F.

Rub the chicken pieces with the lemon halves. Mix together the olive oil, wine, thyme, rosemary, dill, celery, fennel, parsley and salt and pepper. Coat the chicken pieces with this mixture and place in a cas-serole with a cover. Add the garlic cloves and the bay leaf. Cover the casserole and wrap it tightly in aluminum foil. Bake for 1 hour to 1 hour and 15 minutes.

Unwrap the foil carefully, uncover the casserole, turning the lid away from you, and discard the bay leaf. Serve immediately, with lightly toasted slices of French bread. Encourage your guests to squeeze the garlic out of its skin and spread it on the French bread.

Baked Garlic (with a Little Chicken) and Spicy Tomato and Onion Salad

Roast Chicken with Lemon Honey Butter

Serves 4–5

¾ cup sage or clover honey
½ pound unsalted butter
juice of 1 lemon
a 3½- to 4-pound roasting chicken
salt and freshly ground black pepper

In a small saucepan, heat the honey over medium heat, but do not allow it to boil. Remove from the heat and add the butter, a little at a time, stirring to incorporate each addition. Add the lemon juice and let cool slightly.

Lightly sprinkle the chicken with salt and pepper. Place the chicken in a dish just large enough to hold it snugly. Coat the chicken with the honey sauce, inside and out. Cover the chicken and let marinate in the refrigerator for 4 hours.

Preheat the oven to 450°F.

Transfer the chicken to a roasting pan and recoat it with some of the honey butter left in the marinating dish. Save the rest of the marinade for basting. Bake the chicken, breast side down, for 10 minutes.

Turn the chicken over, baste with more of the honey mixture and roast for 10 minutes more. Lower the oven heat to 350°F and continue turning the chicken and basting it every 15 minutes or so for 1 hour to 1 hour and 15 minutes.

Remove the chicken to a heated platter and skim off the fat from the roasting pan. Cook the pan juices on top of the stove over high heat until they thicken, scraping to loosen any particles sticking to the pan. Pour the juices over the chicken or serve in a gravy boat. (This is a good gravy for mashed potatoes.)

Guinea Hens with Wild Rice Stuffing

Serves 6

⅓ cup uncooked wild rice
⅓ cup uncooked brown rice
4 tablespoons unsalted butter
3 celery stalks with leaves, chopped
1 large or 2 small onions, chopped
2 fennel ribs, chopped
salt and freshly ground black pepper
6 guinea hens or rock Cornish game
    hens (about ¾ pound each)
olive oil or Garlic Oil (page 19)

Soak the wild rice in cold water for 1 hour. Soak the brown rice in a separate bowl for the same amount of time. Rinse the rices and place in separate pots, in plenty of cold water. Bring to a boil and simmer, covered, for 40 minutes. Drain.

In a large, deep-sided sauté pan, melt the butter and in it lightly sauté the celery, onions and fennel until the onions become transparent. Add the drained rices and toss to mix thoroughly. Season to taste with salt and lots of fresh pepper. Remove from heat and allow to cool slightly.

Preheat the broiler.

Lightly brush the hens with a little of the oil. Divide the slightly cooled rice mixture evenly among the cavities of the hens. Place the hens on a broiling rack, breast side down. Broil a few inches from the heat for a few minutes, until the skin begins to brown. Turn the hens on their sides and broil until they begin to brown. Repeat on the remaining sides until done, about 20 minutes total.

Serve with a simply prepared green vegetable, such as steamed asparagus or broccoli, and my Carrots in Orange Juice (page 188).

Turkey Tonnato

This is my answer to the more expensive dish *vitello tonnato*. Substituting a whole turkey breast for the veal is a novel and easy way to present a tasty, cold summer dinner or luncheon. Turkey breast is 98 percent fat-free, and while it doesn't taste like veal, it's very good in its own right. The tuna sauce completes this inexpensive dish that is elegant enough to serve at a very fancy gathering. *Serves 8*

*1 whole turkey breast, ribs attached
     (about 5 pounds)*
1 onion, quartered
1 carrot, peeled and halved
2 celery stalks, halved
3 peppercorns
3 sprigs parsley

TONNATO SAUCE

*two 6½-ounce cans white tuna packed
     in oil, drained*
1 tablespoon fresh lemon juice
2 tablespoons chopped parsley or dill
1 cup mayonnaise
*½ cup cold chicken stock (homemade if
     possible, unsalted if canned)*
⅛ teaspoon cayenne pepper
2 tablespoons drained capers

Place the first six ingredients in a small stockpot and cover with cold water. Bring to a boil, reduce heat, and simmer, skimming occasionally, for 40 minutes. Remove from heat and allow turkey to cool in its own broth. When completely cool, remove turkey from broth, wrap well, and refrigerate for 3 hours or overnight.

Shortly before serving, debone turkey breast and wipe it clean with paper towels. Slice crosswise into ½-inch slices. Arrange on a platter and pour tonnato sauce evenly over the slices.

In a blender or the work bowl of a food processor fitted with the steel blade, combine all the Tonnato Sauce ingredients except the capers. Blend or process until smooth. Pour the sauce over the turkey slices and garnish with the drained capers.

Duck with Cranberry Stuffing & Sauce

As much as I like turkey, I get tired of seeing it at every Christmas dinner. For a change of pace I sometimes serve this duck at Christmas, as well as at other times. It's a fun replacement for Old Tom. *Serves 6*

two 4- to 5-pound fresh ducklings
Cranberry Stuffing (below)
salt and freshly ground black pepper
2 cups dry white wine

With a large needle, prick the ducklings in several places in the fatty parts. Plunge the ducklings into a large pot of rapidly boiling water and allow to boil for 10 to 15 minutes. (This is to release some of the fat. Boil longer if there still seems to be a great deal of fat.) Remove the ducklings from the water and let cool.

Preheat the oven to 450°F.

Pat the ducklings completely dry, inside and out. Loosely stuff them with the slightly cooled Cranberry Stuffing and season the skin with salt and pepper. Place the ducklings breast side up on a rack in a roasting pan and roast for 20 minutes.

Lower the oven heat to 350°F. Using a bulb baster or spoon, carefully skim off and discard the hot fat from the pan. Add the wine. Continue to roast the ducklings, basting frequently with the pan juices, for 1½ hours. Remove from oven and allow to rest for 15 minutes before carving. Serve with Raw Cranberry Sauce.

Cranberry Stuffing

I like using fresh cranberries whenever I can get them, and it saddens me that you can usually only find them between Thanksgiving and Christmas. So if I'm lucky enough to find them past New Year's, I use them as often as possible. Loosely pack a roasting chicken with this stuffing or bake the stuffing in a covered, buttered casserole and serve it as an accompaniment to lamb or beef. Or use it to stuff the center of a crown roast of pork. This recipe makes enough for two ducklings or one large roasting chicken or crown roast of pork; double the recipe for turkey.

½ cup unsalted butter
3 tablespoons finely chopped onion
3 tablespoons chopped celery
1½ cups chopped raw cranberries
4 tablespoons brown sugar
2 teaspoons freshly grated gingerroot
¾ teaspoon salt
½ teaspoon ground mace
1½ teaspoons fresh chopped thyme, or
    ½ teaspoon dried
¼ teaspoon freshly ground black pepper
grated rind of 1 orange (no white pith)
4 cups fresh soft breadcrumbs

In a large, deep-sided sauté pan, melt the butter over medium heat and in it sauté the onion and celery until the onion is soft and transparent. Do not brown. Remove from heat and stir in the cranberries and brown sugar.

In a mixing bowl, combine the ginger, salt, mace, thyme, black pepper and orange rind with the breadcrumbs. When thoroughly mixed, add to the sauté pan and cook for 4 to 5 minutes over medium heat, stirring frequently. Allow to cool slightly before stuffing a turkey or duck. When stuffing a crown roast of pork or lamb, mound the stuffing in the center and cover with aluminum foil until the last half hour of cooking. Or cook the roast for 1 hour, remove from oven, stuff the center and return to oven for the remainder of the cooking period.

Raw Cranberry Sauce

I serve this every Thanksgiving, in place of canned or homemade cooked cranberry sauce. It's also good with chicken and pork.

4 cups raw cranberries, picked over
3 oranges, peeled and chopped (no white pith)
about 1¼ cups sugar
2 tablespoons grated fresh gingerroot

In a blender or food processor fitted with the steel blade, chop the cranberries coarsely. Add the chopped oranges, sugar and grated ginger and process until just combined.

Christmas Goose with Fruit & Pecan Stuffing & Port Gravy

In Europe at Christmastime, goose is the bird of choice. I first tasted goose cooked this way in Gstaad, Switzerland, at the home of some very dear friends. The stuffing has pieces of mixed dried fruits—apricots, prunes, raisins, nectarines, pears—that soak in a good port. More port is added to the pan drippings to make a scrumptious gravy. The flavors of the fruit and port complement one another, but you could easily substitute a good Madeira, another fine fortified wine, in both the gravy and the stuffing. Or try pear brandy if you'll be using dried pears in the stuffing, peach brandy if you're using peaches, and so on. Feel free to experiment— I do, even with favorite recipes. It makes the dish more your own.

Most of the geese you find in the markets today will be frozen. Be sure to give your poultryman one or two weeks' notice, and he can surely get you one. Plan to pick up the goose two or three days in advance, leave it in its plastic wrapping and let it slowly thaw on the bottom shelf of your fridge. This slow-thaw method causes the least deterioration of texture. I do the same thing with frozen turkey.

Dubbed the most versatile bird in the world, the goose provides us with down and feathers for parkas, pillows and those puffy warm quilts called duvets. Its liver gives us the elegant and expensive *pâté de foie gras,* and the not-so-elegant-but-no-less-treasured strained goose fat for cooking. As you can see, the goose is a highly prized bird. And when cooked properly, it makes a delicious and unusual dinner.

Serves 6

Christmas Goose with Fruit and Pecan Stuffing and Port Gravy, Braised Fennel, and Chive Potatoes

a 12-pound goose

GIBLET STOCK

giblets from the goose
1 large onion, halved and quartered
2 large carrots, chopped
4 sprigs parsley
4–5 black peppercorns
1 bay leaf
1½ quarts chicken stock (homemade if possible, unsalted if canned)

STUFFING

4 tablespoons unsalted butter
¾ cup chopped shallots or onions
2 cups chopped dried fruit (any combination of pitted prunes, chunks of dried apricots, nectarines, pears or raisins), steeped for 6 hours or overnight in
1½ cups old port (the best you have)
3½ cups bread chunks, from good French bread
3 Granny Smith or pippin apples, peeled, cored and chopped
1½ cups chopped pecans or pine nuts
4 tablespoons chopped (flat-leaf) Italian parsley
2 teaspoons fresh oregano, or 1 teaspoon dried
salt and freshly ground black pepper to taste

PORT GRAVY

¼ cup unbleached all-purpose flour
2½ cups giblet stock
1¼ cups old port
salt and freshly ground black pepper to taste

PREPARE THE GIBLET STOCK

Place the giblets, onion, carrots, parsley, peppercorns, bay leaf and chicken stock in a saucepan and bring to a boil. Skim off and discard any surface scum. Reduce the heat to low, cover partially and simmer very gently for about 2½ hours. Strain the stock through a sieve lined with a kitchen towel that has been well rinsed to remove any detergent residue. Skim off the fat and reserve the stock.

Plunge the goose into a very large pot of boiling water. Boil for 15 minutes, to release some of the fat. Drain and pat completely dry, inside and out. Cover the goose and set aside. (If you wish to save the goose fat, skim it from the hot water and reserve. Covered and refrigerated, it keeps for about a month.)

In a small skillet, melt the butter and sauté the shallots or onions until soft and transparent. Do not brown. Transfer the contents of the pan to a large bowl and let cool 5 minutes. Add the macerated fruit and port, the bread chunks, apples, pecans, parsley and oregano. Mix thoroughly. Add salt and pepper to taste.

Loosely stuff the goose through the neck. Truss it as you would a turkey. Put the remaining stuffing in a well-greased casserole dish with a cover and set aside. Prick the skin of the goose all over with a needle or long fork to help release fat during roasting.

Preheat oven to 400°F.

Place the goose breast side up on a rack in a roasting pan and roast for 25 minutes. Remove pan from oven and turn the goose breast side down. (To avoid burns, always remove pan from the oven when moving the goose.) Return the goose to the oven, reduce the heat to 325°F, and place the casserole of stuffing in the oven to be cooked as long as the goose. After 1 hour, remove the roasting pan from the oven, turn the goose breast side up, and roast for 1 more hour. Remove the goose fat from the pan with a bulb baster or large spoon frequently during roasting. (If you desire, you can save the goose fat, covered and stored in the refrigerator for up to a month.)

When the juices of the goose run clear when the leg is pierced with a long fork, the goose is done. Transfer it to a heatproof platter, turn off the oven, and return the goose to the turned-off oven for 15 minutes while you make the gravy. (Leave the oven door ajar.)

Prepare the port gravy: Skim off as much fat as possible from the juices in the roasting pan and scrape the bottom to loosen any particles. Pour the juices into a saucepan and place over a low flame. Stir in the flour. Very slowly, add the reserved giblet stock and then the port. Bring to a boil, reduce heat, and simmer for 10 to 15 minutes, stirring constantly, until the gravy thickens slightly. Add salt and pepper to taste, strain and pour into a gravy boat. Garnish the goose as desired and bring to the table with the gravy boat.

Meat

"*I* don't eat red meat." I've heard it said a hundred times. I've said it a hundred times myself! (There was a four-year period in my life when I didn't eat meat.) It's been the "fashion" lately to forgo meat. We've heard all the reasons: animal fat, cholesterol, it's tough to digest and so on. My heart, my arteries. My eye! A little meat once in a while is just fine, assuming your doctor has not forbidden it.

Few foods have the protein value of meat. Besides, it's delicious and satisfying. After four meatless years I ate a perfectly broiled T-bone steak. Yum, I loved it. I had heard all the stories: "It may make you sick," "Your body won't be able to take it." Rubbish! In fact, when I finished eating it, I felt great. Beef, lamb, pork—they're wonderful. The key, in food as in life, is moderation. Enjoy meat occasionally, prepared simply and without rich sauces. Balance the fat content of your entire meal by steaming your veggies, and eliminate salad oil that night, using only balsamic vinegar as your dressing. Serve fruit for dessert. I wouldn't exactly consider that type of menu a cardinal sin. Remember, we can have *anything* we want, we just can't have *everything* we want!

Carpet Bag Steak

Steak & Peppers

This recipe works equally well with chicken, veal or shelled shrimp. It's a one-pan dish. I use a large, deep-sided copper sauté pan that I take from the stove to the table. *Serves 6*

olive oil
2 red, 2 yellow and 2 green bell peppers, *cut into 1-inch cubes*
3 large white onions, *cut into 1-inch cubes*
4 garlic cloves, *crushed*
2 pounds mushrooms, *thickly sliced or quartered*
four or five 1- 1¼-inch-thick New York steaks (8–10 ounces each), *trimmed of all fat and cut into 1¼-inch cubes*
salt and freshly ground black pepper to taste
½ cup good dry sherry
chopped parsley for garnish

Cover the bottom of a large, deep-sided sauté pan with olive oil, place over very low heat, and add the peppers and onions. Cover and cook, stirring occasionally, for 30 to 35 minutes. Do not allow to brown. Raise the heat to medium-low, add the crushed garlic and mix thoroughly. Add the mushrooms and more oil if necessary. Stir and cook for 3 to 4 minutes, until heated through. With a slotted spoon, remove the pepper mixture to a warm platter.

Raise the heat, add the steak chunks and lightly brown on all sides. Lower the heat, return the pepper mixture to the pan and season to taste with salt and pepper. Stir well. Warm the sherry in a small saucepan. When the pepper mixture is completely heated through, pour in the warm sherry. Simmer for a few minutes, until the sherry is slightly reduced.

Serve on a heated platter, garnished with the chopped parsley. Rice or noodles are good accompaniments.

Prime Rib of Beef with Five Peppers

Don't forget to save the rib bones to make soup stock at another time. If you don't wish to use the bones right away, freeze them in a plastic bag; they will keep well for up to three months. It's a good idea to save up a lot of bones and then make a large amount of stock. Allow the stock to cool, uncovered, and then freeze it in premeasured half- and one-cup amounts for convenience. *Serves 12–14*

Prime Rib of Beef with Five Peppers and Creamed Horseradish Sauce, Puréed Rutabaga, and Tomatoes Stuffed with Puréed Lima Beans

4 garlic cloves
a 10-pound standing rib roast
5 teaspoons Five-Pepper Mélange (page 10), freshly ground
1 teaspoon salt
Creamed Horseradish Sauce (page 112)

Peel the garlic and cut it into narrow slivers. With the tip of a sharp knife make incisions, the same length as the garlic slivers, all over the fatty parts of the beef. Insert the garlic slivers into the incisions. Rub the roast all over with the freshly ground Five-Pepper Mélange and salt, patting it on, until the meat and fat are thickly covered. Place the roast rib side down in a roasting pan. Cover with waxed paper and allow to stand at room temperature for 1 hour.

Preheat oven to 500°F.

Place the pan on the middle rack and roast for 30 minutes. Lower the heat to 350°F and continue to cook for 1½ to 2 hours, depending on how you like your beef cooked. (To get a true reading, use a meat thermometer inserted into the fleshy center of the roast where it will not hit a rib bone or fat: 120–125°F for rare meat, 125–130°F for medium-rare, 135°F for medium and 150°F for well done.) Remember that the center will be rarer than the end pieces. Remove the roast from the oven and transfer it to a heated platter. Allow to rest for 15 to 20 minutes before carving.

Meanwhile, pour off all of the fat from the pan, reserving the pan juices. Scrape the bottom of the pan to loosen the brown bits. Pour the juices into a heated gravy boat. Carve the roast and add the meat juices to the gravy boat. Serve immediately, with the horseradish sauce.

Creamed Horseradish Sauce

Ten years ago I planted one horseradish root. I now have a permanent, good-sized patch. This recipe is for my favorite creamed horseradish sauce. I think the butter I use in it pops out the flavor of the horseradish.

2½ tablespoons unsalted butter
2½ tablespoons all-purpose flour
¼ teaspoon salt, or to taste
¾ cup chicken stock (homemade if possible, unsalted if canned)
⅓–½ cup freshly grated horseradish
1 cup whipping cream

In a small, deep-sided saucepan, melt the butter over medium heat. Gradually stir in the flour and salt. Cook over low heat for a couple of minutes, stirring; do not allow to brown. Gradually stir in the chicken stock and the grated horseradish and bring to a simmer. Slowly stir in the whipping cream, and stir continuously with a whisk or large spoon until thick and creamy.

Serve with any cut of beef or lamb. I also like this sauce with salmon or swordfish.

Carpet Bag Steak

This is the type of hearty dish that was served in the Old West to the likes of Wild Bill Hickok and Buffalo Bill. I'm sure carpet bag steak was one of their favorites. I have visions of wooden tubs of oysters packed with ice being carried by the fastest horses to Buffalo Bill's favorite restaurant. *Serves 6*

24 shucked raw oysters, brought to room temperature
3 green onions, sliced, or ⅓ cup chopped fresh chives
6 to 10 drops Tabasco sauce, or to taste
3 tablespoons unsalted butter, cut into tiny pieces
salt and freshly ground black pepper to taste
1 whole New York strip steak (3¼–4 pounds)

Preheat broiler.

In a glass bowl, mix together the oysters, onions, Tabasco sauce, butter and salt and pepper to taste.

With a sharp knife, cut a deep horizontal pocket (about 4 to 5 inches deep) into the thicker side of the steak. Fill the pocket with the oyster mixture and sew together with a large needle and thick trussing thread. Place on a shallow pan. Broil 2 to 3 inches from the flame, turning once—12 to 14 minutes per side for medium-rare to medium, 14 to 16 minutes per side for medium to medium-well done. If you want the meat well done (I hope you don't), brush after 15 minutes with a little melted butter and brush again as needed to keep it from drying out.

Remove steak from broiler and transfer to a heated platter. Pull out the thread and pour the pan juices over the steak. Carve into individual servings at the table and spoon some oysters over each portion.

Beef Cabernet Sauvignon

This beef recipe calls for 3 cups of my favorite California wine, Cabernet Sauvignon. Many labels are widely available; choose the best you can afford. (My favorite is Jordan.) Don't worry about serving a recipe with so much wine to children. The alcohol evaporates during the long cooking time, leaving behind an incredible flavor. This is the reason I use wine, spirits and liqueurs so often in my cooking.

If you want to add veggies other than the ones called for in the recipe, go ahead. I would suggest cut-up green beans, turnips, pitted black or green olives (added during the last 10 minutes of cooking), even raw corn kernels. However, I've given you the recipe as I like it best. *Serves 6*

3 pounds stew beef, such as rump, chuck or top round, trimmed of fat and cut into 1½-inch cubes
1 tablespoon all-purpose flour
1 teaspoon salt
1 teaspoon freshly ground black pepper
1 teaspoon sweet paprika
3 tablespoons olive oil
1½ tablespoons unsalted butter

3 cups dry red wine, preferably a California Cabernet Sauvignon
1½ cups beef stock (homemade if possible, unsalted if canned; if unsalted is unavailable, omit the salt in this recipe)
4 garlic cloves, minced
1 tablespoon fresh thyme leaves, or 1 teaspoon dried
1½ tablespoons tomato paste

1 bay leaf
1 pound pearl onions
1 pound carrots, peeled and sliced ¼ inch thick
½ pound shelled fresh peas (or a 10-ounce package frozen peas, thawed and drained)
6 celery stalks, sliced ¼ inch thick
1 pound small mushrooms
chopped parsley for garnish (preferably Italian flat leaf)

Pat the beef cubes dry with paper towels. Mix together the flour, salt, pepper and paprika in a large bowl and toss the beef cubes in it to coat them evenly. Heat the olive oil and butter in a large skillet or deep-sided sauté pan over medium-high heat until hot, but not smoking. Add the beef a few pieces at a time and brown on all sides. (Don't add all the beef cubes at once, or they won't brown properly.) As the beef cubes are browned, transfer them to a large plate with a slotted spoon. Pour off and reserve the fat remaining in the skillet. Add the wine and 1 cup of the beef stock to the skillet. With a large spoon or spatula, dislodge all the brown bits clinging to the bottom of the pan. Heat, but do not allow to boil, and stir in the minced garlic, thyme and tomato paste. Return the beef and any juices to the pan. Add the bay leaf. If there is not enough liquid to cover the beef, add the remaining ½ cup beef stock and more wine, if necessary. Bring to a boil, cover, immediately reduce the heat to low and let simmer for 3 hours. Occasionally skim off any surface fat, stir and replace the lid.

Bring a large pot of water to a boil and add the pearl onions. When the water returns to a boil, remove the onions with a slotted spoon. When they are cool enough to handle, carefully remove the skins. Cut an X in the root ends so they won't come apart during further cooking. Return the water in which you cooked the onions to a boil. Add the sliced carrots and the shelled peas. (If using frozen peas, do not add them yet.) Return to a boil and cook for 4 to 5 minutes. Add the sliced celery and cook 2 minutes more. Drain the vegetables and pat dry with a towel. In a medium-sized, deep-sided sauté pan, pour enough of the reserved oil to cover the bottom. Over medium heat, lightly brown the parboiled vegetables and the whole mushrooms. Remove from the pan with a slotted spoon and stir the veggies into the beef stew. (If you are using frozen peas, add them now.) Remove the bay leaf and continue to simmer for another 15 minutes or so. Garnish with the chopped parsley and serve.

Steak au Poivre Mélange

Serves 4

*four 1- 1¼-inch-thick New York steaks
    (about 8–10 ounces each)*
*8 tablespoons coursely ground Five-
    Pepper Mélange (page 10)*
⅓ cup unsalted butter
⅓ cup olive oil or Garlic Oil (page 19)
⅓ cup cognac
½ cup dry red wine
*½ cup beef stock (homemade if possible,
    unsalted if canned)*

Place the steaks on a large platter lined with waxed paper and press the ground peppers onto all sides. In a large, deep-sided iron skillet or sauté pan, melt the butter with the oil over high heat. Add the steaks and sear quickly on both sides. Cook to the desired degree of doneness, 5–6 minutes per side for medium-rare, 6–7 minutes per side for medium, longer for well done. Transfer the steaks to a heated platter and set aside.

In a small saucepan, warm the cognac. Add the wine and beef stock to the sauté pan. Bring to a simmer and let cook for 1 to 2 minutes. Add the warm cognac and continue to cook, stirring, until the alcohol has burned off, about 2 minutes. Pour the sauce over the steaks and serve at once.

Calf's Liver with Sage

Serves 6

6 thin slices of calf's liver (about 1
* pound)*
all-purpose flour for dredging
6–8 tablespoons unsalted butter
½ cup dry white wine
1 tablespoon chopped fresh sage
whole sage leaves for garnish (optional)

Dust the calf's liver on both sides with the flour. Melt 6 tablespoons of the butter in a large sauté pan over medium heat. Add the liver slices and cook for 2 to 3 minutes on each side. Transfer the liver to a heated platter.

Add the wine to the pan and scrape loose any brown bits clinging to the bottom. Let simmer for 2 to 3 minutes. Add the fresh sage. For a rich sauce, you may add a tablespoon or two more butter. Pour the hot sage sauce over the liver slices and garnish with the whole sage leaves, if desired. Serve at once.

Calf's Liver Swiss Style

Serves 4

8 strips sugar-cured bacon

4 tablespoons unsalted butter

¼ cup olive oil or Garlic Oil
   (page 19)

4 large white onions, sliced

1 pound calf's liver, cut into 1½-inch
   strips

12 cherry tomatoes, halved

In a heavy skillet, fry the bacon until crisp and remove from pan; drain between paper towels.

Melt the butter with the oil in a medium-sized, deep-sided sauté pan over medium-high heat. Add the sliced onions and cook, stirring, until they are well browned, about 15 to 20 minutes. Reduce heat to medium, and add the liver pieces, cherry tomatoes and more oil, if necessary. Cook the liver for a few minutes only, turning frequently. It should still be pink in the center. (If you overcook, the liver will be tough and the cherry tomatoes will disintegrate.)

Transfer the liver, onions and tomatoes to heated plates. Garnish with the bacon slices and serve at once, with boiled potatoes.

Veal with Orange

To keep the veal tender, this recipe must be executed very quickly. I've made the orange liqueur optional. The dish is good without it, but *great* with it. *Serves 4*

8 veal scallops or medallions, pounded
    flat
flour for dredging
salt and freshly ground black pepper to
    taste
½ cup unsalted butter
1 beef bouillon cube, mashed
juice of 1 orange, squeezed shells
    reserved
2 tablespoons orange liqueur (optional)
2 oranges, peeled, sliced crosswise thinly
    and seeded
¼ cup finely chopped parsley for
    garnish

Dredge the veal lightly on both sides in the flour and sprinkle with salt and pepper to taste. Melt the butter over medium-high heat in a large sauté pan. Add the mashed bouillon cube, stir to dissolve, and add the veal. Sauté for 1 minute on each side. Pour in the orange juice, add the orange shells and cover the pan for 1 minute. Quickly transfer the veal to a heated serving platter and keep warm.

Discard the orange shells and return pan to the heat. Add the orange liqueur, if desired, and simmer for a moment. Add the orange slices and heat through. Arrange the orange slices around the veal and pour the sauce over all. Garnish with the parsley and serve at once.

Veal Paprika

Serves 6

4 tablespoons unsalted butter

3 pounds boneless veal, cut into 1-inch
    cubes

3 large white or yellow onions, chopped

4 garlic cloves, minced

1 large red or yellow bell pepper, seeded
    and chopped, with several rings of
    red or yellow pepper for garnish

3 large tomatoes, peeled, seeded and
    chopped

1/2 teaspoon sweet paprika, or to taste

salt and freshly ground black pepper to
    taste

1 cup water

1/2 cup dry sherry

In a large, deep-sided sauté pan melt the butter over low heat. Add the veal, onions, garlic and chopped pepper and sauté over medium heat for 7 to 8 minutes. Add the tomatoes, paprika, and salt and pepper to taste. Mix thoroughly and stir in the water and sherry. Bring to a simmer, cover the pan and allow to simmer gently, stirring occasionally, for 1 hour. Garnish with the red or yellow pepper rings.

Serve with lightly buttered egg noodles and a green veggie.

Ham Steaks with Rum Raisin Sauce en Papillote

Serves 4

½ cup raisins
⅔ cup dark rum or port
½ cup unsalted butter
4 cooked ham steaks, each about ½ inch thick
½ cup sour cream

Soak the raisins in the rum or port for 3 hours, then drain, reserving the rum or port (you should have about ½ cup left). Set aside.

Preheat oven to 400°F.

In a large sauté pan, melt the butter and in it sauté the ham steaks over medium heat until browned on both sides. Add the reserved port or rum and cook for 5 minutes. Remove from heat.

Using a pair of scissors, cut large rectangles from parchment paper. Place a ham steak on one half of each rectangle.

Stir the sour cream into the pan juices remaining in the sauté pan. Add the raisins and pour the sauce, dividing it evenly, over the steaks. Fold the other half of the rectangles over and roll the edges to seal them tightly, forming envelopes. Place in a baking pan. Bake for 10 minutes.

To serve, place the parchment packages on individual heated plates and slash through the center of each.

(You may cut large heart shapes instead of rectangles; seal as above.)

Paper Bag Ham with Figs in Sauternes

Years ago I was served a dessert of fresh peeled figs sitting in a champagne glass filled with Sauternes. It was a combination of flavors I've never forgotten. I enjoy baking in parchment paper, but when I decided to experiment with ham and figs in Sauternes I was forced to come up with a larger paper container, and discovered a new use for the brown paper bags you get at the supermarket. Try baking a turkey in a paper bag, too. *Serves 10–12*

2 pounds dried figs
about 2 cups Sauternes
light vegetable oil
6 bay leaves
a 6- to 8-pound sugar-cured or honey-
  baked precooked ham
12 fresh figs, quartered, for garnish
  (optional)

Place the dried figs in a bowl, add enough Sauternes to cover and let macerate, covered, for 6 hours or overnight.

Preheat oven to 300°F.

Using a pastry brush, lightly coat the entire inside surface of a large paper bag with vegetable oil. Place the bag on its side in a large, deep roasting pan. In the bottom of the bag, make a bed of macerated figs and bay leaves. Place the ham on top and pour in the Sauternes. Twist or tie the opening or fold the edges over and staple them.

Bake until the ham is heated through, about 2 hours. (Follow the directions on the package or can.) Remove pan from oven. To avoid a blast of hot steam in your face, open the bag away from you using a sharp knife or scissors. Transfer ham to a heated platter. Remove and discard the bay leaves. Surround the ham with the cooked figs. Slice and serve, garnished with quartered fresh figs if desired.

IMPORTANT NOTE: Do not use a recycled paper bag, as it will give off noxious fumes when heated. (Most recycled bags are labeled as such; if in doubt, ask—or don't use.)

Sweet-and-Sour Roast Pork

Since this is a roast, I like to serve it with my Chive or Shallot Potatoes. Also, a green veggie is called for here and I suggest you try my recipe for Creamed Spinach. *Serves 6–8*

a 4-pound pork rib roast, center cut
2 cups white sugar
1 cup white vinegar
1 cup and an additional 2 tablespoons water
1 teaspoon salt
1 tablespoon each of finely chopped red, yellow and green bell peppers
4 teaspoons cornstarch
2 teaspoons paprika
¼ cup chopped fresh cilantro (also called Chinese parsley or coriander)

Preheat oven to 450°F.

Place the pork roast bone side down in a roasting pan, and roast for 30 to 35 minutes, or until nicely browned.

Meanwhile, prepare the sweet-and-sour sauce: Combine the sugar, vinegar, the 1 cup of water, salt and chopped peppers in a medium saucepan. Bring to a simmer over medium heat and cook for 5 minutes. In a small mixing bowl, combine the cornstarch with the 2 tablespoons of water to make a smooth paste. Add this to the saucepan and cook over low heat, stirring constantly, until thickened.

Strain the sauce through a sieve into a bowl and work the solids through with the back of a spoon. Stir in the paprika and the chopped cilantro.

Lower oven heat to 300°F. Transfer the meat to a deep-sided baking pan or dish. Pour the sweet-and-sour sauce evenly over the pork roast and return to the oven, basting with the sauce every 15 minutes or so, for 2½ hours.

Remove the roast to a warm platter and let rest for 10 to 15 minutes before slicing. Pour the hot sauce remaining in the pan over the slices or serve in a sauceboat. Serve at once.

Ginger Pork Ribs

Eating ribs is much more fun if you cut them properly. By properly, I mean cutting off the excess bones to leave meat on both sides of each rib. You will be left with several extra bones. Throw them away and enjoy. *Serves 8*

8–10 pounds baby back pork ribs, in
    manageable lengths
2 tablespoons unsalted butter
2 medium white onions, finely chopped
½ cup soy sauce
⅓ cup honey
⅓ cup good dry sherry
2 tablespoons grated fresh gingerroot
a 16-ounce jar ginger preserves or mar-
    malade
2 tablespoons grated orange rind

Place ribs in a bowl or container large enough to accommodate them snugly. Set aside.

In a deep saucepan, melt the butter over medium heat. Add the chopped onions and sauté for 5 minutes, or until transparent. Stir in the remaining ingredients and heat through; do not boil. Remove from heat and let cool.

Pour the cooled sauce over the ribs, turning to coat them evenly. Cover and refrigerate, turning occasionally, for 4 hours.

Grill ribs over hot coals until well browned and cooked through (about 30 minutes), turning several times, and basting frequently with the marinade. (You can also bake them in the oven at 350°F for 30 to 40 minutes, or until browned and cooked through. If they seem to be browning too quickly, cover with foil.)

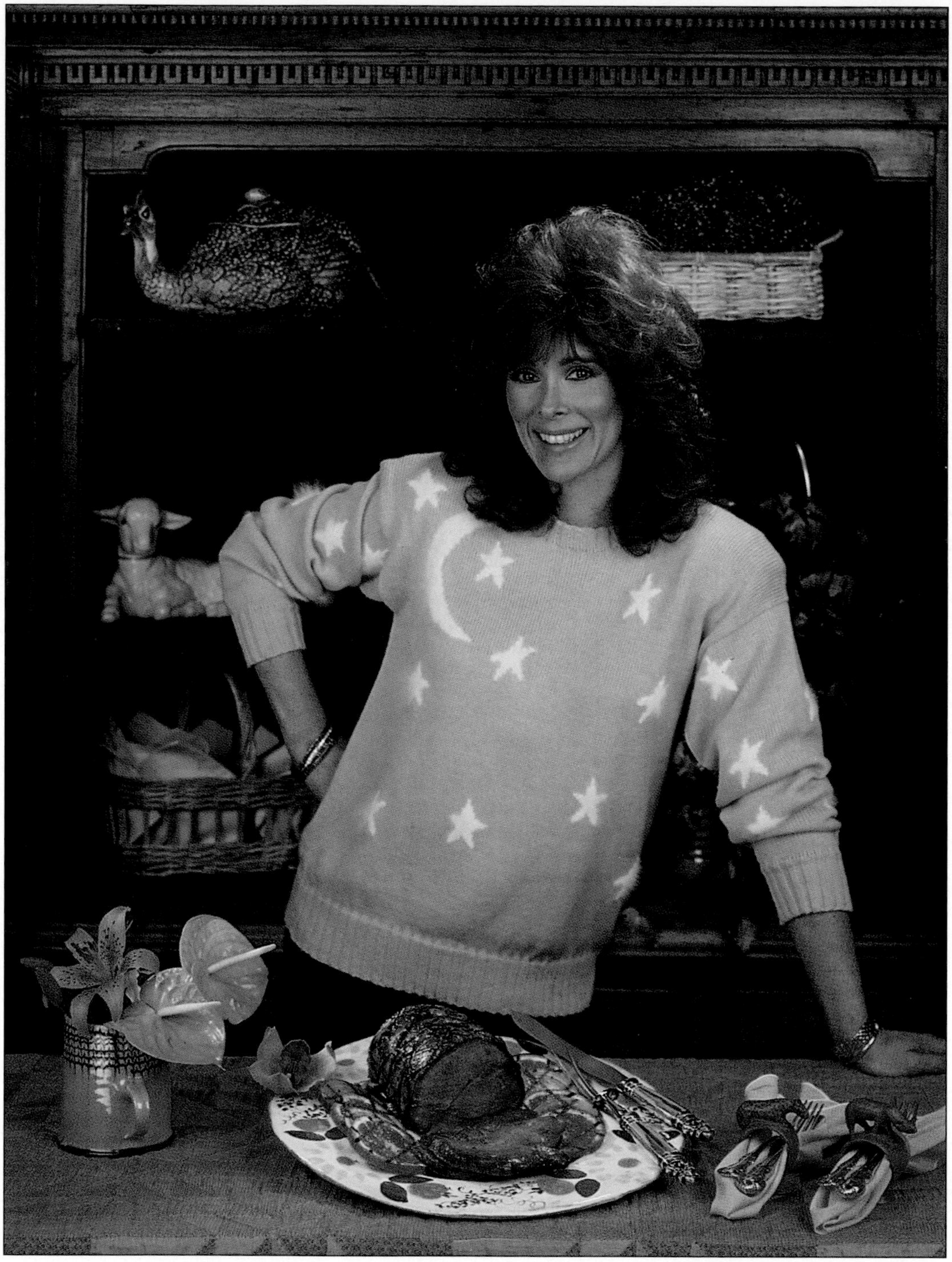

Barbecued Pork Loin with Grilled Onions & Oranges

Because I'm lucky enough to live in Aspen, I have had many opportunities to go camping. The best trip I ever took was the four days and nights I spent with friends floating down the Colorado River in rafts. Each person was responsible for one meal, either breakfast or dinner, and cooking became sort of a competition. (Our lunches were always sandwiches and fruit eaten on the rafts.) When it was my turn, I made this barbecued pork loin with grilled onions and oranges. You will need a grilling basket for the onions and oranges even if you barbecue this in your backyard.

Campfire cooking is a wonderful way for a group of friends or a family to share a meal in the beauty of natural surroundings. But to enhance your enjoyment and that of others you must understand and follow the basic rules of safety as well as good campfire cuisine: Don't smoke in fire danger areas, period. Always build your campfire away from overhanging tree limbs and tall grasses. Arrange the coals in a mound so that the center of the grilling rack is hottest and the sides are cooler, giving you two cooking temperatures. Keep a container of water handy to douse a spark. Use a shovel to bury a fire if it starts. Wait about half an hour for the fire to get hot enough—the coals should be turning gray.

My feelings on littering and souvenir-hunting are best summed up by the sign at Maroon Lake, just under the magnificent Maroon Bells near Aspen: TAKE ONLY PHOTO-GRAPHS; LEAVE ONLY FOOTPRINTS. *Serves 8*

---

2 tablespoons grated orange rind (no white pith)
8–12 ounces Italian salad dressing (bottled or packaged and prepared according to directions)
1 pork loin (about 4 pounds)
3 large red onions, peeled and sliced ¼ inch thick
4 large navel oranges, peeled and sliced ¼ inch thick

Add the grated orange rind to the Italian dressing. Place the pork loin, onion and orange slices in a container large enough to hold them comfortably, pour the dressing over and marinate, turning occasionally, for 1 to 2 hours. (You may have to marinate the pork loin, and onion and orange slices in separate containers. A sealable plastic bag is great for the orange and onion slices, and a very large one would be great for the pork loin, if you are camping.)

Place the pork loin in the center of an oiled rack over hot coals. Sear the pork loin for a minute or two on all sides to seal in the juices. Move the pork loin to the side of the rack, where the coals are not so hot. Grill for 10 minutes on each of all four sides (for a total of 40 minutes or until the internal temperature reaches 145°–150°F on a meat thermometer), spooning the marinade over the loin each time you turn it. Remove from the fire and let rest for 10 minutes before carving.

While the pork is resting, place the orange and onion slices in an oiled grilling basket and place over the fire. Grill, pouring any remaining marinade over them, for about 3 minutes on each side.

Slice the pork loin and serve with the onion and orange slices.

Jalapeño Marinated Lamb Chops

Serves 4

1 cup dry white or red wine
1 tablespoon finely chopped jalapeño
    chili pepper
3 garlic cloves, minced
2 tablespoons white or red wine vinegar
½ teaspoon salt
1 tablespoon chopped fresh thyme, or 1
    teaspoon dried
1 tablespoon chopped fresh rosemary, or
    1 teaspoon dried
8 loin lamb chops, 1–1½ inches thick
2 tablespoons olive oil

In a glass bowl, mix together the first 7 ingredients. Pour this marinade into a glass pan deep enough to hold the lamb chops snugly. Add the chops, turn to coat, and let marinate covered, in the refrigerator, turning them occasionally, for 6 hours or overnight.

Allow the chops to stand in the marinade at room temperature for about 1 hour. Heat the olive oil in a large, deep-sided sauté pan over medium-high heat. Add the lamb chops, reserving the marinade, and cook for 5 minutes on each side. Add the reserved marinade, bring to a simmer and let cook over medium-low heat for 3 to 5 minutes, or until cooked to desired degree of doneness. Transfer chops to a heated platter. Reduce sauce slightly over high heat and pour over the chops. Serve immediately.

Rack of Lamb

MARINADE

2½ teaspoons Dijon mustard
2 garlic cloves, minced
1½ teaspoons olive oil
¾ teaspoon chopped fresh thyme, or ¼
    teaspoon dried, crumbled
¾ teaspoon chopped fresh rosemary, or
    ¼ teaspoon dried, crumbled
pinch salt and freshly ground black
    pepper

6 pounds rib rack of lamb, trimmed of
    all but a thin layer of fat (have your
    butcher "french" the bones)
4 tablespoons unsalted butter
4 teaspoons minced shallots
2 garlic cloves, minced
½ cup stale breadcrumbs
1 tablespoon finely chopped parsley
1 teaspoon fresh chopped thyme, or ⅓
    teaspoon dried, crushed
1 teaspoon fresh chopped rosemary, or
    ⅓ teaspoon dried, crushed
pinch salt and freshly ground black
    pepper

Combine the marinade ingredients in a small mixing bowl. Rub the mixture all over the rack of lamb, cover and let it marinate overnight in the refrigerator.

Return lamb to room temperature. Preheat the oven to 500°F.

In a sauté pan over medium heat, melt the butter and add the minced shallots and garlic. Cook, stirring often, until soft and transparent. Do not allow to brown. Remove from heat and stir in the breadcrumbs, parsley, thyme and rosemary. Add the salt and pepper. Transfer the mixture to a plate. Place the rack of lamb fat side up in a baking pan or dish and place it in the oven for not more than 10 minutes. Remove the lamb, cover the rib bones with foil if they are starting to blacken, and firmly pat the breadcrumb mixture in a thick layer on the lamb fat.

Reduce the oven heat to 400°F and bake the lamb for 10 minutes more. Remove the foil from the rib bones and transfer the lamb to a hot platter. Let rest for 6 to 7 minutes before serving. Slice into individual chops at the table.

Leg of Lamb with Rosemary & Garlic

Serves 6–8

a 5- to 7-pound leg of lamb
*4 garlic cloves, peeled and cut into
    small slivers*
½ head garlic
*1 bunch fresh rosemary, chopped, or
    2–3 tablespoons dried*
*salt and freshly ground black pepper to
    taste*

Preheat oven to 350°F.

With the tip of a sharp knife make many tiny incisions all over the lamb and insert the garlic slivers in the slits. Slice off the top of the half head of garlic and rub the cut side all over the lamb. Rub the lamb with the rosemary; try to insert some into the garlic pockets. Sprinkle the lamb with a little salt and pepper.

Bake the lamb in a roasting pan, basting frequently with the pan juices. (Allow 14 minutes a pound for medium-rare—140°F on a meat thermometer.) Remove from oven and allow to rest for 10 minutes before carving.

Serve with Crème de Menthe Jelly (page 4).

Lamb Roasted with Honey & Rosemary

Lamb and rosemary are a perfect pairing. By adding orange juice, soy sauce and honey, you get a salty-sweet herbal bouquet. Of course, I can't resist adding a little ground ginger. I like to serve this with two or three veggies and my Lemon & Orange Rice. *Serves 8*

1 cup freshly squeezed orange juice
¼ cup light soy sauce
3 tablespoons honey
*1 tablespoon fresh chopped rosemary, or
    1 teaspoon dried*
½ teaspoon ground ginger
¼ teaspoon salt
¼ teaspoon freshly ground black pepper
*a 6- to 7-pound leg of lamb, boned,
    rolled and tied (about 3½ pounds
    after boning)*

Combine the first 7 ingredients in a glass bowl. Place the lamb in a dish large enough to hold it snugly. Pour the marinade over, cover and refrigerate, turning several times, for 12 hours.

Allow lamb to reach room temperature. Preheat oven to 450°F.

Transfer lamb to a roasting pan, reserving the marinade. Place the lamb in the oven to sear for 15 minutes. Lower the heat to 350°F, and roast, basting with the marinade every 10 minutes or so, for 1 hour more.

Lamb Roasted with Honey and Rosemary, Lemon and Orange Rice, Creamed Spinach, and Carrots in Orange Juice

Pasta

The very word *pasta* conjures up warmth and satisfaction. Do you know anyone who doesn't like pasta? I certainly don't. It's my very favorite food. Children who are problem eaters rarely turn it down. It's my very favorite food—but I've already said that, haven't I?

But pasta has been maligned. Everyone thinks it's fattening—everyone but the Italians, that is. How is it possible that the Italians can enjoy pasta once or twice a day, every day, and not weigh 700 pounds? I can offer a couple of explanations. Italian pastas (and some domestic pastas) are made from golden durum semolina wheat that has been washed many times. Washing eliminates excess starch. So semolina flour should be indicated on the label of whatever brand of pasta you buy. The easiest way to see if your brand of pasta has too much starch in it is to put a quantity of it into a large pot of boiling water. If, after a few minutes, the pot threatens to boil over with mounds of starchy foam, you know that your pasta has not been made with washed wheat.

Besides having a lot less starch, golden durum semolina wheat pasta contains no fat. So your fat consumption will only come from what you put into your sauce. Italians rarely serve meat sauce. Meat with pasta is just as fattening as meat and potatoes—the combination of protein and complex carbohydrate will pack on the pounds. And however you prepare the pasta, remember to have normal-sized portions; you can't be a piggie.

Homemade pasta is good, but not as nutritious if it is made from processed bleached white flour; it also contains eggs, which make it higher in cholesterol than manufactured pasta. Another reason I'm not particularly fond of homemade pasta is that it cooks very quickly, too quickly often to know when it has reached a true *al dente* stage. Those who prefer can also now purchase whole-wheat pasta. I've never found a substitute for the imported Italian hard-wheat pastas.

Pasta Primavera

Pasta Primavera

Sirio Maccioni, owner of New York's Le Cirque restaurant, is single-handedly responsible for the popularity of pasta primavera. It is a specialty of that great restaurant. To my own version I add bay shrimp. Substitute Italian sausage for the shrimp if you like. *Serves 6–8*

1¼ pounds imported semolina linguine
   or spaghetti
½ cup pine nuts
4 tablespoons olive oil or Garlic Oil
   (page 19)
4 tablespoons unsalted butter
2 or 3 garlic cloves, minced
3 cups assorted spring vegetables, cut
   into julienne strips and/or small
   pieces (snow or sugar snap peas,
   asparagus, green beans, zucchini,
   crookneck squash, red, green or yellow bell pepper, mushrooms, peas
   or fresh corn kernels)
⅓ cup light or heavy cream
½ cup chopped fresh basil, plus 12–16
   whole leaves for garnish
12 cherry tomatoes, halved
1 pound tiny Oregon bay shrimp,
   cooked
¼ cup chopped Italian flat-leaf parsley
freshly grated Parmesan

Bring a large pot of salted water to a boil. Add the pasta and cook until just *al dente*. Drain well and transfer to a heated serving bowl.

Meanwhile, in a small sauté pan, lightly brown the pine nuts in 1 tablespoon of the oil. Remove with a slotted spoon and set aside; reserve the oil from the pan.

Melt the butter with the remaining 3 tablespoons oil over medium heat, in a large deep-sided sauté pan. Add the oil from the pine nuts, lower the heat, and in it lightly sauté the garlic until soft. Add the pine nuts and the vegetables and lightly sauté, tossing the vegetables until they are almost tender. Add the cream, basil and tomatoes and cook until the tomatoes are heated through.

Add the cooked shrimp. Pour the sauce over the hot pasta, garnish with the chopped parsley, whole basil leaves and grated Parmesan cheese and serve at once.

Pasta with Cherry Tomatoes
à la Cecca

This fresh uncooked sauce is sweet with cherry tomatoes, fragrant with basil and aromatic with raw garlic. (The garlic cloves in the fresh or uncooked sauce are left whole to discourage anyone from eating them.) It's perfect as a first course or as an entrée. You can make the sauce in about 10 minutes, practically ignore it for an entire day, and have dinner ready in the time it takes to cook the pasta. Serve with a large green salad and fresh fruit for dessert. *Serves 6*

2 pints cherry tomatoes, halved
12 garlic cloves, peeled and left whole
pinch of salt and freshly ground black
  pepper to taste
pinch of sugar
2 tablespoons chopped fresh basil
1 pound thin semolina pasta, such as
  spaghetti
6 whole basil leaves for garnish

Mix together the first 6 ingredients and let stand, covered, stirring once or twice, for at least 2 hours to allow flavors to develop.

Bring a large pot of salted water to a boil. Add the pasta and cook until just *al dente*. Drain well and transfer to a heated serving bowl. Pour the sauce over the hot pasta and garnish with the whole basil leaves.

Rigatoni with Vodka Sauce

Serves 4–6

½ tablespoon dried crushed hot red
    pepper plus additional for garnish
    (optional)
½ cup vodka
1 pound rigatoni
a 28-ounce can whole Italian plum
    tomatoes, drained
½ cup chopped fresh basil
4 tablespoons unsalted butter
½ cup whipping cream or half-and-half
freshly grated Parmesan
whole basil leaves for garnish

Allow the dried pepper to steep in the vodka in a glass jar overnight. Strain the vodka, reserve it and discard the pepper.

Bring a large pot of salted water to a boil, add the rigatoni and cook until almost *al dente*.

Meanwhile, place the tomatoes in a large, deep-sided sauté pan and break them up with a spoon over medium heat. Allow to cook for a few minutes until slightly reduced. Add the chopped basil and immediately remove the pan from the heat. Transfer the sauce to a bowl.

Drain the rigatoni.

In the sauté pan, melt the butter over medium-high heat and add the rigatoni, tomato sauce, vodka and cream. Toss continuously until well mixed. Serve immediately, with freshly grated Parmesan and a few whole basil leaves for garnish. A small bowl of crushed red peppers may be served on the side, for those who like it even fierier.

Pasta à la Chèvre

Serves 6

1 pound thin imported semolina pasta,
  such as spaghetti
8 ounces chèvre, *crumbled*
²⁄₃ cup milk
6 tablespoons unsalted butter, melted
½ teaspoon salt
1 cup whipping cream
²⁄₃ cup freshly grated Parmesan cheese
½ red bell pepper, roasted, peeled and
  cut into julienne strips (page 177)
2 tablespoons chopped fresh tarragon or
  basil for garnish
2 tablespoons pine nuts, toasted for
  garnish

Bring a large pot of salted water to a rolling boil. Add the pasta and cook until just *al dente*.

Meanwhile, combine the *chèvre*, milk, melted butter and salt in a large pan over medium heat. Mash the *chèvre* with a fork and stir until creamy, about 1 minute. Remove from heat.

Drain the cooked pasta.

Return the pan to the stove and stir in the cream over low heat. Add the cooked pasta, Parmesan and roasted pepper, and mix well. Serve on a heated platter and garnish with the tarragon or basil and the toasted pine nuts.

Pasta Carbonara

This is my favorite pasta recipe. It's a classic, hearty peasant dish. In my version, I've added mushrooms and onions. But then, I can never follow any recipe exactly, even my own. *Serves 10–12*

2 pounds thin imported semolina pasta, such as thin fettuccine, linguine, or spaghetti

2 pounds sugar-cured bacon, cut into 2-inch pieces

olive oil

1 pound white onions, cut into 1-inch dice

2 tablespoons unsalted butter

1½ pounds mushrooms, sliced (halve them first if large)

8 eggs

1 cup whipping cream or half-and-half

½ cup freshly grated Parmesan

⅔ cup chopped Italian flat-leaf parsley plus additional for garnish

¼ teaspoon dried Italian red peppers, crushed, plus additional for garnish

Bring a large pot of salted water to a boil. Add the pasta and cook until just *al dente*.

Cook bacon, but do not let it get too crisp. Drain between thickness of paper towels, removing as much grease as possible. In a large sauté pan, pour in enough oil to cover the bottom of the pan. Cook the onions over medium heat until soft. Do not brown. (Add more oil if necessary.) Drain between thicknesses of paper towels, removing as much oil as possible. In the same pan, melt the butter and in it cook the sliced mushrooms until almost tender. Do not overcook. Return the onions and bacon to the pan. Mix well and reduce heat to low.

In a bowl, beat the eggs with cream, Parmesan, parsley and crushed peppers.

Drain the pasta. Transfer it immediately to a large preheated bowl or pasta dish. Put the bacon-mushroom-onion mixture over the pasta. Pour the egg mixture over the top and toss until all the strands are coated. (The egg mixture will cook on contact with the hot ingredients, creating a creamy sauce studded with the onions and hot peppers.) Sprinkle with more chopped parsley if desired. Serve with a bowl of grated Parmesan and a small bowl of crushed peppers. Beware, the peppers are very hot!

Processor Pesto

I was taught to make pesto by my first ski teacher, an Italian. I still have his recipe, in which every fourth word is "PEST" in bold letters—*pest* being Italian for "grind." In those days, pesto was made with a mortar and pestle—a time-consuming job. Because of the bother, I rarely made it. A food processor can make it in seconds, and as I always keep pots of fresh basil growing in my greenhouse, I make it often and encourage you to do the same. *Enough for 4–6 servings of pasta*

2 cups fresh basil leaves
4 garlic cloves, minced
1/3 cup freshly grated Parmesan
3 tablespoons pine nuts
1/2 cup olive oil
salt to taste
whole basil leaves for garnish
*1 pound hot cooked pasta such as spa-
    ghetti*

Place all the ingredients, except the whole basil leaves for garnish, in the work bowl of a food processor that has been fitted with the steel blade. Process until you have a smooth paste.

Store in a glass jar, covered with a thin layer of olive oil. Keeps a week or more, tightly sealed in the fridge.

To serve, bring to room temperature and place over hot pasta. (Allow 3–4 tablespoons per serving.) Toss well. Garnish with whole basil leaves and serve with a bowl of freshly grated Parmesan.

Pasta à la Gorgonzola

I've found that Gorgonzola is the best of all blue cheeses for a hot sauce. It seems to have the perfect creamy consistency when heated.

Don't cook the Gorgonzola too long or over too high heat, though, as it will turn stringy. *Serves 6*

1 pound imported semolina pasta, such as fusilli or thick spaghetti
8 ounces Gorgonzola
⅔ cup milk
6 tablespoons unsalted butter, melted
1 teaspoon salt
1 cup whipping cream or half-and-half
⅔ cup freshly grated Parmesan
10 walnuts, freshly shelled and chopped

Bring a large pot of water to a rolling boil, add the pasta, and boil until just *al dente*.

Meanwhile, put the Gorgonzola, milk, melted butter and salt into a large pan and place over medium heat. Mash the Gorgonzola and stir until creamy, about 1 minute. Remove pan from heat.

Drain the cooked pasta.

Return sauce to low heat and stir in the cream. Add the pasta and the Parmesan and mix well.

Transfer to a large, preheated pasta bowl and top with the chopped walnuts.

Pasta al Capitano

Please don't serve grated cheese such as Parmesan with this shellfish pasta. It would absolutely ruin the taste of the delicate sauce. Not all pastas are enhanced by the addition of cheese, and this is definitely one of them. *Serves 8*

1½ pounds thin semolina pasta, such as fettuccine or spaghetti
½ cup unsalted butter
½ cup olive oil
1 large onion, chopped
1 cup dry white wine
6 large garlic cloves, minced
1 teaspoon fresh rosemary, or ⅓ teaspoon dried, crushed
1 pinch fresh or dried oregano
a 28-ounce can Italian plum tomatoes, drained and chopped
3 cups cooked shellfish (shrimp, lobster, scallops, lump crab meat)
½ cup minced Italian flat-leaf parsley
½ teaspoon sugar
salt and freshly ground white pepper to taste

Bring a large pot of salted water to a boil. Add the pasta and cook until just *al dente*. Drain well and transfer to a heated serving bowl.

Melt the butter with the oil in a large sauté pan over medium-high heat. When the mixture is bubbly, add the onion and sauté until golden. Add the wine, garlic, rosemary and oregano. Cook, stirring, until wine has evaporated and butter is golden, but not brown. Reduce heat to medium and add drained tomatoes. Add the shellfish, parsley, sugar and salt and pepper to taste. Stir until seafood is just heated through. Serve over the hot pasta.

Pizza

Pizza is right up there with pasta when it comes to food that is fun, comforting and filling. Children seem to know this instinctively. No matter how fussy they are, they will almost always eat pizza.

Pizza dough is very easy to make in a food processor or by hand. I always add ¼ cup or more of chopped fresh herbs to the flour before I process the dough, choosing them to complement the toppings. For example, I use thyme for my shrimp and scallop pizza, basil for my eggplant pizza, and cilantro for my Mexican pizza. The herbs are certainly optional, but once you've tried them, I don't think you will want plain pizza crust again. Go easy on the herbs if you are cooking for children, though. It may be too sophisticated a taste for them.

*P*izza dough must be given time to rise properly; it should double in bulk, which usually takes an hour or so. To shape it, place the dough on a floured board and, with a rolling pin, roll out the dough as far as you can. Then flour your hands and, starting in the center, pull and stretch the dough to the desired size and shape. Take care not to stretch the center too thin. Of course, you may try to toss it in the air like the pros, but I hope it doesn't land on your head, as almost happened to me.

Vegetarian Pizza

Herbed Pizza Dough

Makes one 12-inch crust

1 package active yeast

1 teaspoon sugar

⅞ cup warm water (about 110°F)

½–¾ cup fresh herb sprigs, such as basil, oregano, Italian flat-leaf parsley, dill, thyme, rosemary or cilantro

2¼ cups + 1 tablespoon all-purpose flour

¼ teaspoon salt

1 tablespoon or more olive oil or Garlic Oil (page 19)

oil and cornmeal for pan

In a bowl, stir together the yeast, sugar and warm water and let stand until foamy, about 10 minutes.

In the work bowl of a food processor fitted with the steel blade, chop the herbs. Turn off the machine. Add the flour and salt. Turn the machine on and off a couple of times. With the machine running, add the yeast mixture, process a few seconds and add the oil. Process until the dough forms a ball at the side of the bowl. Then process for 30 to 40 seconds more.

If you don't have a food processor, chop the herbs finely by hand and toss them with the flour and salt in a large bowl. Make a well in the center and pour in the yeast mixture and oil. Work with a spoon or by hand until all ingredients are combined and a smooth, slightly elastic ball of dough is formed.

Transfer the dough to a bowl that has been rubbed with olive oil and turn to coat the entire surface. Cover the bowl with a damp towel and allow the dough to rise in a warm, draft-free place for 1 hour, or until doubled.

Preheat oven to 425°F.

Roll and stretch the dough out on a lightly floured surface to a 12-inch circle. If the dough is too elastic, try tossing it from hand to hand to flatten it out. Lightly grease the pizza pan with a little oil and sprinkle it with cornmeal. Place the dough on the pizza pan and trim the edges. Bake for 10 minutes on the bottom shelf. Remove from oven and lightly brush the crust with a little more oil. Cover with the sauce and topping of your choice (see the following recipes), and proceed according to the pizza recipe.

Herbed Pizza Sauce

Makes enough for four to six 12-inch pizzas

2½ cups chopped white or yellow onions

4 garlic cloves, minced

5 tablespoons olive oil or Garlic Oil (page 19)

two 28-ounce cans Italian plum tomatoes, drained

a 6-ounce can tomato paste

1 teaspoon sugar

3 tablespoons chopped fresh basil, tarragon, oregano, dill, rosemary, Italian flat-leaf parsley or thyme, or a combination, or a total of 1 tablespoon dried

salt and freshly ground black pepper to taste

In a large, deep-sided sauté pan, sauté the onions and garlic in the oil over medium heat until the onions are transparent. Do not brown. Break the tomatoes up with a spoon and add them to the onions. Mix together the tomato paste, sugar, and the chopped fresh herbs and stir in. Add salt and pepper to taste. Lower the heat and simmer, stirring occasionally, for 30 to 40 minutes. Let cool before using.

Quick Herbed Pizza Sauce

This sauce is a quickie. I don't always have the time to make my own sauce, so I dress up the "store-bought" variety. In addition to garlic, I use thyme for a shrimp pizza, basil for an eggplant one, cilantro for Mexican and so on. Oregano, dill, chives and Italian parsley are also all good herbs to enhance your sauce. *Makes enough for two 12-inch pizzas*

1 garlic clove, minced
1–2 tablespoons olive oil
¼ cup finely chopped fresh herbs of
    choice
a 16-ounce jar prepared pizza sauce
freshly ground black pepper (optional)

In a medium saucepan, sauté the garlic in the olive oil over medium-low heat until soft. Add the herbs, then lower the heat and slowly stir in the jar of pizza sauce. Bring to a simmer and remove from heat. Add pepper, if desired. Allow to cool before using. Add freshly ground pepper if desired.

Vegetarian Pizza

This recipe is a great way to get your kids to eat their veggies. Feel free to add any veggies you like. *Makes one 12-inch pizza*

⅓ cup each of red, yellow and green bell
peppers, cut into ½-inch pieces
2 tablespoons olive oil or Garlic Oil
(page 19)
8 mushrooms, sliced
Herbed Pizza Dough (page 156), made
with oregano
cornmeal for pizza pan
1 cup grated mozzarella cheese
¾ cup Herbed Pizza Sauce (page 157),
made with oregano
⅓ cup sliced black olives

Preheat oven to 425°F.

In a medium saucepan, slowly cook the pepper pieces in the oil over low heat until half done, about 10 minutes. Drain peppers on paper towels and reserve the oil.

In a bowl, lightly toss the sliced mushrooms with 1 teaspoon of the reserved oil until they are well coated; set aside.

Roll out and stretch the prepared pizza dough on a floured surface to a 12-inch circle. Lightly grease the pizza pan with a little of the reserved oil and sprinkle with cornmeal. Place the pizza dough on the pan and trim the edges. Prebake as directed on page 156. Remove from oven and brush with a little more oil. Sprinkle with half the mozzarella and all the pizza sauce. Top with the peppers, mushrooms and olives. Sprinkle with the remaining mozzarella. Bake on the lower shelf of the oven for 20 minutes. Serve immediately.

Mexican Pizza

Makes one 12-inch pizza

1 large red bell pepper
1 large yellow bell pepper
½ jalapeño pepper, seeded and very
*   finely chopped, or to taste*
1 large tomato, peeled, seeded and
*   coarsely chopped*
¼ cup chopped fresh cilantro
1 large red onion, chopped
1–2 tablespoons olive oil
½ garlic clove, minced
Herbed Pizza Dough (page 156), made
*   with cilantro*
1 large white onion, sliced
¾ cup Pizza Sauce (page 157), made
*   with cilantro*
½ cup grated Monterey Jack cheese

Preheat broiler. Place the red and yellow peppers on the broiler rack, 3 or 4 inches from the flame. Broil until the skin blisters and starts to blacken. Turn the peppers and broil until all sides are blistered and slightly blackened. Put the peppers into a paper bag and roll up the bag until you have a small package. (The peppers steam slightly inside the bag, which loosens the skins and makes them easier to peel.)

Combine the jalapeño with the tomato, cilantro and red onion. Put this mixture aside.

When the red and yellow peppers are cool enough to handle (about 15 minutes), peel and seed them. Cut peppers into ½-inch pieces.

In a sauté pan, heat the olive oil over medium-low heat, add the garlic, and cook until the garlic is soft. Do not brown. Add the peppers, stir to coat well and cook for 1 minute. Don't overcook.

Preheat oven to 425°F.

Roll out and stretch the pizza dough on a lightly floured surface to a 12-inch circle. Place in pan and prebake as directed on page 156.

Remove from oven and brush with olive oil. Arrange a layer of sliced onion evenly over the crust. Spoon on the pizza sauce. Top with peppers, then the jalapeño mixture. Sprinkle with the Monterey Jack cheese and bake on the bottom shelf of the oven for 15 to 20 minutes, until browned and bubbly. Serve immediately.

Shrimp & Scallop Pizza

This is more of what I call a party pizza. It's elegant and delicious and can be served as an appetizer (in small pieces), a first course, or simply for dinner. A large green salad, this pizza and Lemon Sorbet (page 234) for dessert make up a menu I serve often. *Makes one 12-inch pizza*

2 tablespoons olive oil

2 garlic cloves, finely minced

4 large shrimp, shelled, deveined and
    halved lengthwise

4 large sea scallops (or 12–14 whole
    bay scallops), washed and halved

1 scallion, halved or quartered length-
    wise

Herbed Pizza Dough (page 156), made
    with thyme

cornmeal for pizza pan

8 ounces mozzarella cheese, grated

¾ cup Herbed Pizza Sauce (page 157),
    made with thyme

3 ounces goat cheese, crumbled

Preheat oven to 425°F.

Place the olive oil and garlic in a medium-sized sauté pan and cook over medium-low heat until the garlic is soft. Do not allow to brown. Reduce the heat to low. Pat the shrimp and scallops dry and add them to the pan. Toss the shellfish in the oil to coat them and remove immediately to a plate. (The shrimp will not be cooked through.) Add the sliced scallion to the pan and cook over medium heat for 3 minutes. Remove the scallion and reserve the oil.

Roll out and stretch the prepared pizza dough on a floured surface to a 12-inch circle. Brush the pizza pan with a little of the reserved oil and sprinkle with cornmeal. Place the dough on the pan and trim the edges. Prebake as directed on page 156. Remove from oven and brush the crust with a little more oil. Top the crust with half the grated mozzarella and half the pizza sauce. Scatter the goat cheese, shrimp, scallops and scallion over the top and spoon on the rest of the pizza sauce. Top with the remaining mozzarella. Return to the lower rack of the oven for 15 to 20 minutes. Serve immediately.

Artichoke, Asparagus & Prosciutto Pizza

Makes one 12-inch pizza

*1 small (7-ounce) jar artichoke hearts
    marinated in olive oil*
6–8 asparagus spears
*Herbed Pizza Dough (page 156), made
    with Italian flat-leaf parsley*
cornmeal for pizza pan
3 ounces mozzarella cheese, grated
3 ounces Parmesan, freshly grated
*¾ cup Herbed Pizza Sauce (page 157),
    made with Italian flat-leaf parsley*
*6 thin slices prosciutto, cut in ½-inch
    pieces*

Preheat oven to 425°F.

Thoroughly drain the marinated artichoke hearts, reserving the oil. While the artichoke hearts are draining, blanch the asparagus spears in boiling salted water for 3 minutes. Plunge the spears immediately into ice water to stop them cooking and pat them dry. Place the drained artichoke hearts on paper towels to finish draining, then slice them into quarters.

Roll out and stretch the pizza dough on a floured surface to a 12-inch circle. Lightly brush a pizza pan with a little of the reserved artichoke oil and sprinkle with cornmeal. Place the dough on the pizza pan and trim the edges. Prebake as directed on page 156. Remove from oven and brush with a little more oil. Sprinkle with half of each of the grated cheeses. Spoon on the pizza sauce and top with the asparagus spears, artichoke hearts and prosciutto. Drizzle a little more oil over the top and sprinkle with the remaining cheese. Return to lower shelf of oven and bake for 15 to 20 minutes. Serve immediately.

Jewish Pizza à la Spago

Created by famed chef Wolfgang Puck, Jewish pizza is a specialty of his renowned Spago restaurant in Los Angeles. This pizza is so "in," it's not even on the menu. I really don't know what makes it Jewish, I just know that I love it. My contribution is adding chopped chives to the cream cheese. I also shape the salmon slices like flower petals.

Makes one 12-inch pizza

Herbed Pizza Dough (page 156), made with ¼ cup chopped chives

1 cup cream cheese mixed with ¼ cup chopped chives, at room temperature

6 slices smoked salmon

2 tablespoons fresh Beluga caviar (or more if desired)

additional chives in bunches for garnish

thinly sliced onion rings for garnish (optional)

Prebake the pizza crust as directed on page 156. While still warm, spread with the cream cheese-chive mixture. Lay slices of smoked salmon on top. Roll up a slice or two of the remaining salmon to form a "flower," bending the "petals" outward. Place a circle of the caviar in the center of the pizza and top with the salmon flower. Garnish with the chive bunches and the onion rings, if desired. Slice and serve with ice-cold vodka.

Eggplant Pizza

I'm an eggplant lover. I've found that most people are definite about eggplant; they either love it or hate it. In this and most eggplant recipes I prefer to use the small Japanese Ichiban variety. They taste just like the larger ones, but their smaller size is much more manageable. *Makes one 12-inch pizza*

2 tablespoons olive oil or Garlic Oil
    (page 19)
1 or 2 small Japanese eggplants, sliced
    lengthwise ¼ inch thick
1 medium zucchini, sliced lengthwise,
    ¼ inch thick
Herbed Pizza Dough (page 156), made
    with chopped basil
cornmeal for pizza pan
4 ounces mozzarella cheese, grated
4 ounces Parmesan, freshly grated
¾ cup Herbed Pizza Sauce (page 157),
    made with basil
2 small onions, sliced ¼ inch thick
6 mushrooms, thickly sliced

Preheat oven to 425°F.

Place the oil in a medium-sized sauté pan and over medium-high heat quickly brown the eggplant slices on both sides, for 3 to 4 minutes. Drain on paper towels. Add the zucchini and brown. Drain on paper towels. Reserve the oil.

Roll out and stretch the pizza dough on a floured surface into a 12-inch circle. Brush the pizza pan with a little of the oil and sprinkle with cornmeal. Place the dough on the pan and trim the edges. Prebake as directed on page 156. Remove from oven and brush with a little more oil. Spread with half the mozzarella and half the Parmesan. Cover with the pizza sauce and top it with the sliced onions. Top with the eggplant, zucchini, and mushroom slices and sprinkle the remaining cheese on top. Return to the bottom shelf of the oven for 15 to 20 minutes. Serve immediately.

Vegetables &
Side Dishes

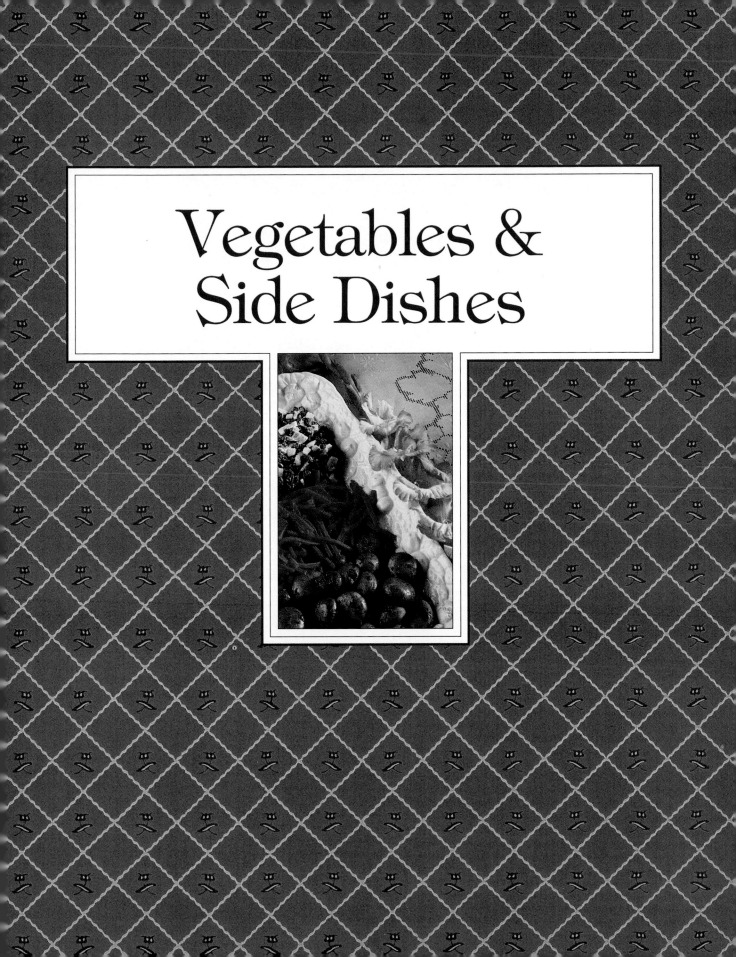

The first thing I did when I moved into my house was to start a vegetable garden. I now have three separate kitchen gardens. One holds my perennial asparagus and strawberries. They are perfect companions, as they bear at different times but benefit equally from applications of old rotted cow manure. The main garden is for vegetables, and like millions of other gardeners I spend some of winter's cold evenings reading seed catalogs, planning next spring's garden. I'm always on the lookout for new and rare seeds to try out. This year I have ordered radicchio. I hope it is successful. The third garden is for herbs. They like sun and a lot of organic fertilizer, and they get it.

I'm a veggie freak, and I confess it shamelessly. My mother says I was the only child she knew who would fix herself a plate of vegetables for breakfast. You may note that she wasn't surprised that I wanted to fix myself breakfast, only that it was made out of veggies. I still love all vegetables. About once a week, I have an all-veggie dinner. My vegetable curry recipe and my vegetable quiche are favorite indulgences.

Puréed Rutabaga

Rutabaga is one of those vegetables that a lot of people have never tasted. What a pity! Try substituting parsnips for the rutabagas. What? You haven't tasted parsnips either?
Serves 12

5 pounds rutabaga
½ cup unsalted butter, cut into pieces

Wash the rutabaga and place them in a large pan of boiling water to cover. Cook over low heat until tender, about 1 hour. (When a fork pierces the center easily, they're done.) Drain and skewer them on a fork. Peel. In this way you don't burn your fingers.

Cut the rutabaga into 2-inch cubes and place them in a food processor fitted with the steel blade. (Or use a potato ricer.) Add the butter to the work bowl and process on and off a couple of times until the butter has been evenly incorporated.

Serve immediately or reheat in the top of a double boiler.

Puréed Lima Beans

This recipe can be made just as easily with peas, corn, carrots, broccoli and so on. When I really want to impress, I hollow out vegetable shells such as pattypan squash, tomatoes or a whole red cabbage and fill them with this purée. (I steam the hollowed-out squash, but leave the tomatoes or cabbage raw.) It really looks pretty. *Serves 6–8*

2 cups chicken stock (homemade if possible, unsalted if canned)
3½ cups freshly shelled lima beans (or substitute frozen beans)
4 tablespoons unsalted butter
4 tablespoons whipping cream
2 tablespoons chopped chives for garnish

In a medium saucepan, heat the chicken stock to the boiling point and add the lima beans. When the stock returns to a boil, reduce the heat and simmer for 15 to 20 minutes, or until the beans are tender. Do not overcook. Drain the lima beans and reserve the stock.

Purée the lima beans in a food processor or blender, adding as much stock as needed to reach the consistency you desire. (Be sure to add the stock slowly, because if you add too much, you will have lima bean soup.) When the purée is smooth, add the butter and the cream. If necessary, reheat the purée in the top of a double boiler over simmering water, stirring frequently.

Serve hot, in hollowed out vegetables, such as steamed pattypan squash or red cabbage halves, or tomatoes. Garnish with the chopped chives.

Roasted Peppers

This versatile dish may be served as an appetizer or as a vegetable side dish. Roasted peppers can also be puréed or sliced for use in sauces, soups and salads. I like to make a pretty presentation of red, yellow and green peppers on a platter. They will sit obediently on a buffet table for hours.

Servings depend on quantity of peppers

Preheat broiler.

Place whole red and yellow bell peppers on the broiler rack, 3 to 4 inches from the flame. Watch them carefully, turning them until the skin is blistered and slightly blackened on all sides. Place the peppers in a paper-grocery bag, and roll the end of the bag to make a tight package. (The peppers steam slightly inside the bag, which will help loosen the skins.)

When the peppers are cool enough to handle, about 15 minutes, peel and seed them. Arrange the peppers on a platter. Serve at room temperature or cover and refrigerate. Olive oil may be drizzled over the peppers before serving, if desired.

Braised Fennel

Fennel looks like short, fat celery with dill on top. It has a fabulous anise scent and, in this braised version, makes an unusual party dish.

I'm a great fan of fennel in all forms. I use it sliced raw in salads. I chop the fern-like leaves and add them to salad dressings, as well as to sauces for fish and chicken. *Serves 12*

8 fennel bulbs
2–3 cups chicken stock (homemade if possible, unsalted if canned)
¾ cup unsalted butter
salt and freshly ground black pepper to taste

With a sharp knife, trim off all the leafy stalks and the base of the fennel bulbs. Chop and reserve 4 teaspoons of the leaves. Cut the bulbs in half lengthwise, then cut them into wedges as you would an apple.

Bring the chicken stock to a simmer in a large saucepan, add the fennel, cover, and cook over low heat until you can pierce them with a fork, about 15 to 20 minutes. Drain the fennel (reserve the stock for another use). Melt the butter in a large skillet and sauté the fennel over medium-high heat until very lightly browned on all sides. (Add more butter if necessary.) Add salt and pepper to taste.

Transfer the fennel to a heated dish. Pour the hot pan juices over and sprinkle with the reserved fennel leaves.

Vegetable Quiche in Herb Pastry

···

Every time I make a quiche it always seems to turn out a little different. That's because different veggies are available at different times. I serve quiche as a nutritious luncheon, and as it holds more veggies, I use a deep quiche pan with a removable bottom, for a handsome presentation. *Makes one 10-inch quiche, to serve 6 as a main course*

···

HERB PASTRY

¼ cup chopped fresh herbs, such as parsley, thyme, tarragon, dill or rosemary, or a combination
1 large egg yolk
¼ cup + 1 tablespoon cold water
½ teaspoon salt
½ cup unsalted butter, very cold
1½ cups all-purpose flour

FILLING

¼ cup freshly grated Parmesan
1¼ cups grated Swiss cheese
4–5 cups sliced or cut-up mixed vegetables such as zucchini, green beans, peas, green onions, asparagus, mushrooms, carrots, cherry tomatoes, chives and red, yellow or green bell peppers)

4 large eggs
1½ cups whipping cream
2 tablespoons all-purpose flour
½ teaspoon salt
⅛ teaspoon freshly ground black pepper
⅛ teaspoon freshly grated nutmeg

Prepare the herb pastry:

Using a food processor fitted with the steel blade, finely chop the herbs. Turn the machine off, add the egg yolk, water, salt and butter. Pulse on and off a few times, then process continuously for 6 seconds. Add the flour and process until the dough just clings together. Do not let it form a ball; if you overprocess the dough it will be tough. (To make the dough by hand, mince the herbs and toss them with the flour and salt in a mixing bowl. Work in the butter with a pastry cutter until the mixture is crumbly. Quickly mix in the cold water and egg yolk, working just until the dough clings together.) Transfer the dough to a plastic bag. Work the dough briefly in the plastic bag until it forms a ball. Flatten the ball and place the bag in the refrigerator for 2 hours or overnight.

Butter a deep 10-inch quiche pan with a removable bottom. On a lightly floured surface, roll the dough into a large 13- to 14-inch circle, about ⅛ inch thick. Fit the dough into the buttered quiche pan, leaving a 1- to 2-inch overhang around the rim. Fold this overhang in, to form a double thickness on the sides. Press the dough firmly in place with your fingertips, gently easing the crust ½ to ¾ of an inch above the rim. Crimp the crust to make a nice edge. Pierce the bottom and sides of the pastry with a fork in several places and refrigerate until firm, about 30 minutes.

Preheat oven to 400°F. Line the pastry with parchment or waxed paper and a layer of pie weights or uncooked dried beans or rice. Bake the shell for 12 minutes. Carefully remove the paper and weights. Pierce the pastry again with a fork and return to the oven for another 6 minutes, or until the pastry is lightly browned. Remove from the oven and let cool before filling.

Lower oven to 375°F.

Fill the shell: Evenly sprinkle half the cheeses over the pastry. Top with a layer of vegetables. Sprinkle with the rest of the cheese and arrange more vegetables on top. (If you are using mushrooms, asparagus or halved cherry tomatoes, save them for this layer.) Combine remaining ingredients in a bowl and mix well. Carefully pour or spoon the egg mixture over the veggies. Do not overfill. Bake for 45 to 50 minutes, or until the custard is set and the top is nicely browned. Remove from oven and place on a wire rack to cool for 10 to 15 minutes, before removing the rim. Serve immediately.

Serve hot or warm.

Lemon Garlic Mashed Potatoes

Serves 8

2 pounds red or white potatoes
1 tablespoon fresh lemon juice
3 or 4 garlic cloves, minced
⅓ cup unsalted butter
1½ teaspoons grated lemon rind
salt and freshly ground black pepper to
  taste
thin lemon slices for garnish (optional)

Cut the potatoes into large chunks. Bring a large pot of water (salted, if you like) to a boil and add the lemon juice and potatoes.

While the potatoes are boiling, gently sauté the garlic in the butter over medium-low heat until soft. Do not brown.

When the potatoes are tender, drain and return them to the pot and warm over low heat for a few minutes, shaking the pot, until the excess moisture has evaporated.

Mash the potatoes lightly with the back of a spoon or a potato masher. Put half the potatoes into the work bowl of a food processor that has been fitted with the steel or plastic blade and add half the garlic butter and half the grated lemon rind. Process on and off 2 or 3 times, then add the remaining potatoes, garlic butter and lemon rind. Process on and off 2 or 3 times more. Don't overprocess the potatoes, or they will become gluey. (You can also mash them by hand or with a potato ricer.) Transfer to a heated serving bowl and add salt and pepper to taste, and serve at once, garnished with the lemon slices, if desired.

Chive or Shallot Potatoes

Don't peel the potatoes. That way you benefit from the potassium in the skins. I also happen to love the taste of potato skins. Don't you? *Serves 8*

2 pounds red potatoes
½ cup unsalted butter, cut into small chunks
6 bunches of chives or 6 shallots, chopped
½ cup half-and-half, heated but not boiled
flowering chives for garnish

Cut the potatoes into large chunks. Bring a large pot of water (salted, if you like) to a boil and add the potatoes. Cook over medium heat until tender. Drain and return them to the pot. Shake the potato chunks for a few minutes over low heat until the excess moisture has evaporated. Mash the potatoes lightly with the back of a spoon or a potato masher.

In the work bowl of a food processor fitted with the steel blade, process the butter chunks and the chives or shallots until the chives or shallots are in tiny pieces and thoroughly incorporated into the butter. Add half the potatoes and process on and off 2 or 3 times. Add the remainder of the potatoes and process on and off. Heat the half-and-half and add. Process on and off once more. (Don't overprocess the potatoes or they will turn gluey.) Transfer to a heated platter and add salt and pepper to taste. Garnish with the flowering chives, if you are lucky enough to find some.

Risotto al Gorgonzola

Gorgonzola, the marvelous Italian blue cheese, just happens to be a great cooking cheese. It melts beautifully, and used in a risotto it's a winner. *Serves 6–8*

6 cups beef or chicken stock (homemade if possible, unsalted if canned)
5 tablespoons unsalted butter
3 tablespoons olive oil
1 large white onion, chopped
2 cups raw long-grain or Italian Arborio rice
4 ounces Gorgonzola, crumbled
3 tablespoons freshly grated Parmesan

Bring the stock to a boil; maintain at a simmer over low heat.

Melt 4 tablespoons of the butter with the oil in a large, deep-sided sauté pan over medium heat. Add the chopped onion, lower the heat slightly and cook until light brown.

Gradually stir in the rice and continue stirring until it becomes translucent. Stir in a cup of the simmering stock; when the rice has almost absorbed it, stir in another cup of stock. Continue adding stock until the rice is tender, and creamy, about 15 to 20 minutes, adding only as much stock as the rice will absorb. Don't let it dry out!

Remove the pan from the heat and stir in the cheeses and the remaining tablespoon butter. Cover the pan and let the risotto stand for a minute or two before serving.

Lemon & Orange Rice

Serves 4–6

1 cup long-grain rice
1 teaspoon grated or finely slivered
  orange peel
1 teaspoon grated or finely slivered
  lemon peel
thin lemon and orange slices for garnish
  (optional)

Mix rice with orange and lemon peels and steam or boil according to directions on package.

Garnish with thin orange or lemon slices, if desired.

Vegetable Curry

This is a terrific all-veggie dinner, or lunch if you prefer. I like a strong curry flavor, but you may wish to reduce the quantity of curry powder to taste. I always find that curry powder "ripens," or gets stronger, after half an hour or so. *Serves 4*

6 tablespoons unsalted butter

6 tablespoons chopped onion

3 tablespoons all-purpose flour

1–2 tablespoons curry powder

6 cups chicken stock (homemade if possible, unsalted if canned)

2 cups cooked vegetables in bite-sized pieces (carrots, peas, squash, eggplant, turnips, artichoke hearts, peppers or mushrooms, and so on)

salt and freshly ground black pepper to taste

1 egg yolk

1 tablespoon fresh lemon juice

GARNISHES

chopped fresh tomato

green, red or yellow bell peppers, seeded and chopped

chopped red onion

peanuts

green apples, peeled, cored, chopped and drizzled with lemon juice to prevent discoloring

raisins

shredded coconut

sliced banana drizzled with lemon juice to prevent discoloring

mango chutney

Melt the butter in a saucepan and add the chopped onion. Sauté over medium heat until soft and golden. Do not brown. Mix together the flour and curry powder and add to the onion. Stir well for 3 or 4 minutes, then slowly add the chicken stock and cook for 15 to 20 minutes, or until the sauce is creamy. Add the cooked vegetables and salt and pepper to taste.

Reduce heat to the lowest setting. When the sauce stops bubbling, stir in the egg yolk that has been preheated with the lemon juice and a little of the hot curry sauce and combine well. (Adding some of the hot curry sauce to the egg yolk mixture first will prevent the sauce from curdling.)

Transfer the curry to a hot platter. Sprinkle the top with any or all of the garnishes. Serve immediately, with steamed or boiled white rice.

Creamed Spinach

Here is a chunky, rather than puréed, version of this old favorite. Be careful not to overcook the spinach. *Serves 4*

¼ cup chopped white onion
4 tablespoons unsalted butter
10 ounces fresh spinach, washed and
    chopped
1 garlic clove, minced
2 teaspoons chopped parsley
4 ounces cream cheese, cut into small
    pieces
1 teaspoon fresh lemon juice
salt and freshly ground black pepper to
    taste
freshly grated nutmeg to taste

In a large saucepan, sauté the onion in the butter over medium-low heat. When the onion starts to become transparent, add the spinach, garlic and parsley and cook for a minute or two over medium heat, stirring until the spinach is limp but still very green. Add the cream cheese, lemon juice, and salt, pepper and nutmeg to taste and blend well. Transfer to a heated platter and serve at once.

**Creamed Spinach,
Carrots in Orange
Juice, Sautéed
Mushrooms in Herbs**

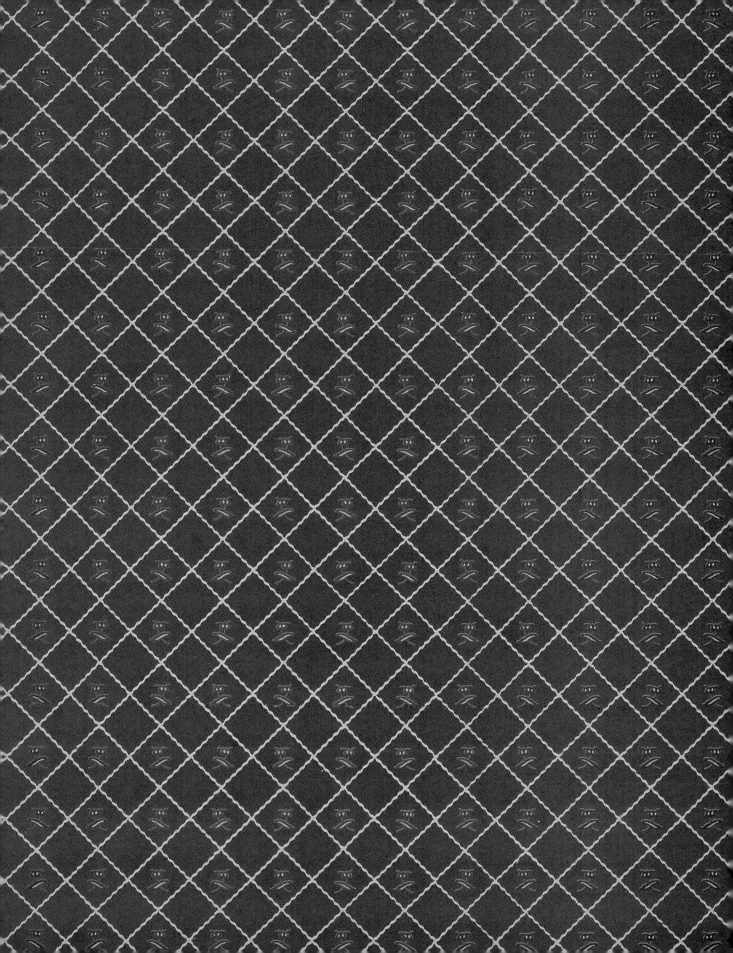

Breads

Like many children, I was given piano lessons. Like many children, I hated them. However, my teacher used to bake bread every day, and I would smell the delicious aroma as I walked up her steps. My prize for a well-completed lesson was a fragrant piece of her still-warm white or wheat bread. I hungered for this, eagerly awaited each piano lesson and diligently practiced my exercises to ensure my rewards. My parents must have thought she was an extremely inspiring teacher. Eventually I started arriving an hour early to learn how she made bread. I learned how yeast was proofed, how to knead and where to put the dough to ensure proper rising. We made white, wheat, egg and rye breads. I can't remember a single piano piece anymore, but that bread will never leave me.

I usually bake six loaves at a time on Fridays. On Monday mornings I would be lucky if there was enough left for toast. I've solved that problem by hiding one loaf! A food processor is the absolute greatest for making bread. Instead of fifteen minutes of hand kneading, you can process most doughs in moments. Don't overprocess, though, or you will have tough bread. I also enjoy batter breads, because you don't have to wait for the dough to rise. Go ahead and try baking bread. Remember, if I can do it, you can do it!

Banana Fruit Bread

Kids love this—big kids too. I like it with morning coffee or at tea time. *Makes 1 loaf*

2 cups sifted all-purpose flour
1½ teaspoons baking powder
½ teaspoon baking soda
¼ teaspoon salt
1 cup mashed ripe bananas
2 eggs, lightly beaten
½ cup unsalted butter, melted
1½ tablespoons buttermilk
1 cup raw sugar
1 teaspoon fresh lemon juice
½ cup chopped dates
½ cup chopped dried apricots
½ cup chopped pecans or walnuts
flour for dusting fruit and nuts

Preheat oven to 350°F.

In a large bowl, sift together the flour, baking powder, baking soda and salt. In a separate large bowl, mix together the mashed bananas, beaten eggs, melted butter, buttermilk, sugar and lemon juice. When the mixture is smooth, gradually stir in the flour mixture. Toss the dates, apricots and nuts with a little flour to prevent them from sinking to the bottom of the batter and stir them in. Mix well.

Pour into a greased 8- × 4-inch loaf pan and bake for 1 hour, or until a toothpick inserted in the center comes out clean. Remove from the pan and let cool on a wire rack.

Banana Fruit Bread, Pecan Bread, Cinnamon-Carrot Bread

Pecan Bread

Makes 1 loaf

2½ cups sifted all-purpose flour
1¼ cups sugar
1 teaspoon salt
2 teaspoons baking powder
2 cups chopped pecans
2 eggs
1 cup milk

Preheat oven to 350°F.

Sift the dry ingredients together into a large bowl and add the pecans.

In a separate bowl, vigorously beat the eggs until they are thick and add the milk. Stir the beaten egg mixture into the flour-nut mixture.

Pour into a lightly greased 8- × 4-inch loaf pan and bake for 1 hour, or until a toothpick inserted in the center comes out clean. Remove from pan and let cool on a wire rack.

Cinnamon-Carrot Bread

By now, most of us have tasted carrot cake, but I like carrot bread. This version has a touch of cinnamon and some chopped pecans for extra taste and texture. *Makes 1 loaf*

¾ cup white sugar
¼ cup brown sugar
¾ cup sunflower oil
2 cups all-purpose flour
1 teaspoon cinnamon
pinch salt
1 teaspoon baking powder
2 eggs, beaten
1 cup grated carrots
½–¾ cup chopped pecans
½ teaspoon Vanilla Extract (commercial or page 11)

Preheat oven to 350°F.

In a large bowl, mix together the sugars and the sunflower oil. Sift the flour, cinnamon, salt and baking powder into the bowl, stopping occasionally to stir the mixtures. Gradually add the beaten eggs until completely combined. Add the carrots, pecans and vanilla and combine well.

Pour the batter into a greased 8- × 4-inch loaf pan. Bake for 1 hour, or until a toothpick inserted in the center comes out clean. Remove from pan and let cool on a wire rack.

Herbed French Bread

When ready to preheat your oven, first place a shallow pan in the bottom and fill it with boiling water. When the oven is fully heated, you will have re-created the steamy atmosphere of the ovens of the French Mediterranean, in which those great crusty loaves that I can't seem to get enough of are baked. *Makes 2 loaves*

1½ cups warm water (105–110°F)
1½ packages active dry yeast
1 teaspoon sugar (I use raw)
3½ cups unbleached all-purpose flour
(I use stone-ground)
⅓ cup chopped fresh parsley, thyme, or
dill, or a combination of all three
2 teaspoons salt
1 teaspoon sugar
beaten egg (optional)

Combine ½ cup of the warm water with the yeast and ½ teaspoon of the sugar and let stand for about 5 minutes, or until foaming. Combine the flour, herbs, salt, the remaining ½ teaspoon sugar and the yeast mixture in the work bowl of a food processor fitted with the steel blade. With the machine running, slowly begin adding the remaining cup of warm water. Let machine run 15 to 20 seconds, adding more flour if dough seems too soft.

Transfer dough to a lightly floured board, and knead, folding the dough toward you and making quarter turns, working in a little flour. Divide the dough in half and shape into long loaves. Generously grease 2 baguette pans with butter and place a loaf in each. Cut three or four diagonal slashes in the tops. Cover with a clean towel and let rise in a warm place for 45 minutes to 1 hour, or until doubled in bulk.

Preheat oven to 450°F, and center a shallow pan of boiling hot water in the bottom of the oven. (For a glazed look, brush the top of the loaves lightly with the beaten egg before baking.) Place the pans on the middle rack over the pan of water and bake for 15 minutes. Reduce heat to 400°F and bake for 15 to 20 minutes, or until the bread is golden brown and sounds hollow when tapped with the flat side of a knife blade.

Granola Bread

This bread is heavy—or hearty—if you prefer. Serve it at breakfast, or simply with coffee or tea. The dough is *so* stiff your food processor may stop. If this happens, simply let the machine cool off for a few minutes and start again. It's well worth the trouble. *Makes 1 large loaf*

1 teaspoon raw sugar
½ cup warm water (110°F)
1 package active dry yeast
2½ cups unbleached flour
½ cup whole-wheat flour
1 cup granola
¼ cup shredded coconut
¼ cup finely chopped dates or raisins
½ cup honey
⅓ cup chopped almonds
1 teaspoon salt
2 tablespoons vegetable oil
1 egg
½ cup warm milk (110°F)

Mix together the raw sugar and the warm water. Sprinkle in the yeast, stir once, and leave to proof. In about 10 minutes, the mixture will have doubled in bulk and be frothy.

In a food processor fitted with the steel blade, place the flours, granola, coconut, dates or raisins, honey, almonds, salt and oil in the work bowl and process on and off until blended to a coarse mixture. With the machine on, add the egg and the yeast mixture through the feed tube. Blend for 10 seconds. Add the warm milk and process 10 seconds more. (Add a little more warm milk or unbleached flour if the dough is too dry or too wet.) Process for about 45 seconds more. Turn the dough out onto a lightly floured surface and knead by hand for 6 or 7 turns. Shape into a ball and place in an oiled bowl, turning several times until the dough is completely coated. Cover with a cloth and allow to rise in a warm, draft-free place until doubled in bulk, about 2 hours.

When the dough has doubled in bulk, punch it down and turn it out onto a lightly floured surface. Cover with a towel and let rest for 10 minutes in a warm, draft-free place. Shape the dough into a fat loaf and place on a greased baking sheet. With a sharp knife, slash the top in a tic-tac-toe pattern. Cover with a towel and let rest in a warm, draft-free place until double in size, about 1 hour.

Preheat oven to 350°F. Bake the bread on the middle rack of the oven for 45 minutes. The loaf is done when it sounds hollow when tapped with the flat side of a knife blade. Remove from pan and cool on a bread rack.

Onion Corn Rye Bread

This bread requires three risings. I usually make it on a weekend so I won't feel rushed. *Makes 2 loaves*

1 teaspoon raw sugar
1 teaspoon light brown sugar
⅓ cup warm water (about 110°F) +
    ¾ cup warm water
2 packages active dry yeast
1 medium onion, coarsely chopped
1½ cups rye flour
1 cup yellow cornmeal
½ cup whole-wheat flour
2 cups + 1 tablespoon unbleached flour
1 teaspoon salt
2 tablespoons caraway seeds
1 tablespoon poppy seeds
¼ cup caraway or white vinegar
6 tablespoons corn or vegetable oil
oil for greasing
1 egg white
2 tablespoons cold water

Dissolve the sugars in the ⅓ cup warm water. Add the yeast and let the mixture stand until it becomes frothy and doubled in volume, about 5 minutes. Place the onion in the work bowl of a food processor fitted with the steel blade and process on and off a few times, until the onion is chopped. Add the rye flour, ½ cup of the cornmeal, the whole-wheat flour, unbleached flour, salt, caraway and poppy seeds and process on and off for 4 or 5 seconds, until all the ingredients are thoroughly mixed.

Pour the ¾ cup warm water, the caraway or white vinegar and the vegetable oil into the yeast mixture, stir once, and, with the machine running, slowly add this mixture to the flours in the processor. Process 30 seconds or so, adding more wheat or white flour if necessary to make a stiff dough. If the mixture is too dry, add 1 or 2 teaspoons warm water and process 2 to 3 seconds more. The dough should form a ball and come away from the sides of the work bowl.

Oil a large mixing bowl and place the dough in it. Turn several times to completely coat the dough with the oil. Oil a piece of plastic wrap and loosely cover the bowl with it. Set the dough in a warm, draft-free place to rise until doubled in bulk, about 2 hours. Carefully remove the plastic wrap and punch the dough down, three or four times. Oil the plastic wrap again, cover the dough, and allow to rise again until doubled, about 2 hours. Remove dough to a clean work surface, punch down and shape into 2 fat oval loaves. Sprinkle a large baking or cookie sheet with ¼ cup of the cornmeal and transfer the loaves to the sheet. Oil several sheets of plastic wrap and loosely cover the loaves with them. Allow to rise as before, one last time, until doubled in bulk.

Preheat oven to 400°F. Beat the egg white lightly with the cold water. Slash the loaves diagonally in a few places with a sharp knife and brush with the egg white mixture. Sprinkle with the remaining ¼ cup cornmeal. Place on the middle rack of the oven and bake for 15 to 20 minutes, then reduce heat to 375°F and bake for about 25 minutes more. Remove from the oven when the loaves sound hollow when tapped with the flat of a knife blade. Remove the loaves to a bread rack and let cool.

Onion Corn Rye Bread, Granola Bread, Pink Grapefruit Oatmeal Bread, Nasturtium Butter

Jalapeño Cornbread

Darlene Vare, who assisted me with the art direction for this book, gives an annual Fourth of July party in Aspen. With the help of the Aspen Fire Department, the city puts on an amazing fireworks and laser show each year on Aspen Mountain. Darlene's garden offers a perfect view of the display. Guests are asked to bring foods that will round out a feast for and by friends. There is much phoning over who is making what. One year, all of us agreed that the cook of one of the guests must give us her recipe for cornbread. Darlene called, but to her surprise the cook refused, saying it was an old family recipe.

After a lengthy conversation, we decided that Darlene should call back, and beg. The next day, she reported triumphantly that the cook had giggled and said, "I was only kidding, here it is." We made the cornbread and it was great but a little soggy. Later, I experimented with different proportions of the ingredients until I liked the consistency.

Two months later, following a trip to the market, I called Darlene. "Remember how hard you had to beg for that cornbread recipe?" "I sure as hell do!" she said. "Well," I replied, "it's on the back of my new box of cornmeal!"

So much for original recipes. (I've since found versions of the recipe in several books.) It seems we all use almost the same ingredients, but in different measurements. I've occasionally added crumbled, cooked bacon and/or crushed, dried chilis to my cornbread. I've baked it in orange and grapefruit shells on the trail, and of course in plain old muffin pans. But here's the way I really like to make them.

~~~~~~

3 canned jalapeño peppers, chopped
1–1½ cups grated sharp cheddar cheese
1½ cups frozen creamed corn, cooked and cooled
1 teaspoon baking powder
½ teaspoon baking soda
1 teaspoon sugar
⅓ cup unsalted butter, melted
¼ cup milk (whole, low- or non-fat)
¾ teaspoon salt

Preheat oven to 400°F.

In a large bowl, mix together half the chopped jalapeños and half the grated cheese with the rest of the ingredients. Stir well and pour or spoon into a greased 9-inch square baking pan. Sprinkle the remaining cheese and jalapeños on top and bake for 40 to 45 minutes, until firm and golden. Turn out on a rack at once, to prevent the cornbread from steaming in the pan. Cut into squares and serve immediately, or wrap in foil and reheat before serving.

Three Cheese Bread

I bake this cheese bread to serve with soup and a green salad for a light but satisfying lunch. *Makes 2 large loaves*

2 packages active dry yeast
8½ teaspoons sugar
2 teaspoons salt
4 cups sifted all-purpose flour
1½ cups low-fat milk
1 tablespoon unsalted butter
½ cup shredded cheddar cheese
½ cup shredded Swiss cheese
½ cup freshly shredded Parmesan (grate it by hand into long shreds)

In a large bowl, lightly mix together the yeast, sugar and salt with 2 cups of the sifted flour.

In a large saucepan, heat the milk and butter over low heat until almost hot (125°F). Use a cooking thermometer. Slowly beat the milk and butter into the dry ingredients and continue to beat for only a couple of minutes. Don't overbeat.

Slowly stir in the 3 cheeses and the remaining 2 cups of flour until the batter is stiff. Cover the bowl and let rise in a warm, draft-free place until dough is doubled in size, about 1 hour.

Preheat oven to 350°F. Using a large plastic or wooden spoon, stir down the batter and transfer it to a well-greased 9- × 5-inch (2 quart) loaf pan. Bake on the middle rack of the oven for 45 minutes, then lay a piece of foil or parchment paper loosely over the top and bake for another 15 minutes. Bread is done when it sounds hollow when tapped with the flat side of a knife blade. Immediately remove the bread from the pan (to prevent it from steaming) and let it cool on a rack.

Pink Grapefruit Oatmeal Bread

Makes 1 large loaf

1 sweet pink grapefruit
½ cup + 2 tablespoons light brown
  sugar
1½ cups all-purpose flour
4½ teaspoons baking powder
¼ teaspoon baking soda
1 cup uncooked rolled oats
2 eggs
2 tablespoons salted butter, melted
⅓ cup water

Preheat oven to 350°F.

Grate 1 tablespoon of the grapefruit rind (no bitter white pith) and set aside. Cut the grapefruit in half, and with a grapefruit knife or spoon, remove segments from one half, taking care to eliminate the white membranes. Cut the grapefruit segments into small pieces and place in a medium bowl with the 2 tablespoons light brown sugar. Mix well. In a large bowl, sift together the flour, baking powder, baking soda and the remaining ½ cup light brown sugar. Mix in the uncooked rolled oats. Lightly beat the eggs with the melted butter and add to the grapefruit pieces. Juice the remaining half grapefruit and measure out ⅓ cup grapefruit juice. Stir into the egg mixture the grapefruit rind, grapefruit juice and water. Stir this mixture into the flour-oatmeal mixture until well blended.

Pour the batter into a greased 9- × 5-inch loaf pan. Bake on the middle rack of the oven for 1 hour, or until a toothpick inserted in the center comes out clean. Turn out and cool on a wire rack.

Herbed Butter

This is good with hot, crusty herbed French bread or dinner rolls. It's also great for buttering sandwiches and tea sandwiches. Or add one minced garlic clove to the butter mixture, roll the butter into a log shape, wrap in plastic and chill. Slice off thin rounds as needed and place on hot cooked meat, chicken or fish. Delicious. *Makes 1 cup*

½ cup finely chopped fresh herbs, such as thyme, chives, dill, parsley and so on, or a combination
½ teaspoon strained fresh lemon juice
1 cup unsalted butter, at room temperature
salt to taste (optional)
herb sprig for garnish

In a small bowl, cream together the chopped herbs, lemon juice and butter. If desired, add salt to taste. Place in a serving crock or dish, cover and refrigerate for 2 hours to allow the flavors to develop.

Garnish with an herb sprig before serving.

Nasturtium Butter

I love to serve nasturtium butter with dinner rolls. An individual crock, garnished with a whole nasturtium flower, is so pretty that even the timid are tempted to try it. Once people taste its peppy flavor, they're hooked. *Makes 1 cup*

4 edible nasturtium flowers (see pages 28, 29), finely chopped
1 cup unsalted butter, at room temperature
1 whole nasturtium flower for garnish

In a small bowl, cream together the chopped nasturtium flowers and the butter. When thoroughly blended, pack into a serving crock or dish. Cover and refrigerate for 2 hours to allow the flavor to develop.

Garnish with the whole nasturtium flower.

Eating in Bed

One of the nicest things you can do for yourself, your family and your friends is to make a big production out of Saturday or Sunday breakfast. Most of us spend the weekdays in a rush, grabbing a cup of coffee and a piece of toast before tearing out the door. But weekends give us a chance to unwind, to enjoy the mornings over a leisurely, special meal. Weekend brunches can also be an inexpensive way to entertain before going on to a sporting or other special event. We have a hunt in Aspen, and the hunt breakfasts are a big event. Tables groaning with food are attacked by hungry horsemen and -women.

My breakfast-brunch suggestions are not quite so excessive. I like to concentrate on an egg dish like *Huevos Rancheros con Salsa* and warm tortillas, Baked Apple Pancake, or

Homemade Swiss Muesli and French Toast with Brandied Lemon Butter. Fresh orange or grapefruit juice and pots of hot coffee and herb tea complete the table. You can entertain a lot of people for about two or three dollars per person this way.

But besides a breakfast party, what could be nicer than crawling back into bed with two breakfast trays filled with my Parsi Scrambled Eggs (a glorious Indian concoction), hot Cinnamon-Vanilla Coffee, the papers and the one you love?

Open-Faced Omelet Paysanne

Homemade Swiss Muesli

I've been fortunate enough to spend a lot of time in Switzerland. *Muesli* is to the Swiss what corn flakes are to us, but like most foods, the homemade kind tastes better. I always include it when serving a fancy breakfast or a large brunch. My recipe incorporates the shredded green apples used by the Dolder Grand Hotel in Zurich, the bananas and strawberries from the version served by the Palace Hotel in Gstaad, and so on. The dates, grapes and almonds are my idea. Make extra, as it goes fast. *Serves 6*

1½ cups whole or non-fat milk

2 cups uncooked oatmeal or rolled oats

*¼ cup oat bran (available in health
    food stores)*

¼ cup grated coconut

*2 Granny Smith or pippin apples,
    peeled, cored and chopped*

juice of 1 lemon

2 tablespoons sugar (preferably raw)

*½ cup halved seedless red or green
    grapes*

½ cup diced dates

½ cup chopped almonds

½ cup raisins or sultanas

1 banana, sliced

1 cup whipping cream

6 strawberries, sliced

In a large mixing bowl, combine the milk with the oatmeal, oat bran and grated coconut. Let stand, stirring once or twice, for about 15 minutes.

Meanwhile, peel, core and grate the apples into a large mixing bowl. Sprinkle them with the lemon juice and toss with the sugar until blended. Add the grapes, dates, almonds, raisins and banana.

Stir the fruit and nut mixture into the oatmeal mixture. Whip the cream until it forms soft peaks and fold half of it into the combined fruit and oatmeal mixture. Spoon the muesli into bowls and garnish each serving with a sliced strawberry and a dollop of whipped cream.

Baked Apple Pancake

One of the specialties of the great Polo Lounge in the Beverly Hills Hotel is its apple pancake. Truly divine! I offer you my version. *Serves 1 or 2*

1 cup all-purpose flour
⅓ cup + ½ teaspoon white sugar
¼ teaspoon salt
1 cup beer, at room temperature
2 egg yolks
4 egg whites, at room temperature
2 Granny Smith or pippin apples,
    peeled, cored and chopped
¼ cup light brown sugar
1½ teaspoons cinnamon
¼ small lemon
3 tablespoons unsalted butter
1 tablespoon vegetable oil
sour cream at room temperature for
    garnish

Preheat oven to 350°F.

Sift together into a large mixing bowl the flour, 1½ teaspoons of the white sugar and the salt. Add the beer and stir until smooth. Beat in the egg yolks, one at a time.

In a separate bowl, beat the egg whites with 1 tablespoon white sugar until they form soft peaks. Fold them into the batter. Peel, core and slice the apples medium thin.

Mix together the remaining ¼ cup of the white sugar, the brown sugar and the cinnamon. Reserve 2 teaspoons of this mixture. Squeeze the lemon over the apples and toss the slices with the cinnamon-sugar mixture until they are well coated.

Heat the butter and oil in a 9- or 10-inch round baking pan, spring-form cake pan or ovenproof skillet. Pour in half the batter and cover with all of the apples. Pour in the remaining batter and bake on the middle rack for 1 hour, or until the pancake is puffed and golden.

Loosen the sides and bottom of the pancake with a metal spatula and slide it onto a hot plate. Sprinkle with the remaining cinnamon sugar. Cut into wedges and, if desired, garnish with a dollop of sour cream.

Huevos Rancheros

Although I now live in Colorado, I was born in Los Angeles, a few hours from the Mexican border. This recipe for *Huevos Rancheros* is the direct result of my Southern California childhood. I was practically weaned on Mexican food, and the Mexican food I am used to—and definitely favor—utilizes fresh homemade salsas, not cooked or canned sauces.

Check a Spanish or Oriental grocery if you have trouble finding fresh jalapeño peppers or fresh cilantro (also called coriander or Chinese parsley). This is an all-or-nothing recipe. If you are unable to find these ingredients fresh, there are really no acceptable substitutes. And heed this warning: After chopping jalapeños or other hot peppers wash your hands well, and keep them away from your eyes, because the pepper's volatile oils can be extremely irritating. (Wearing gloves while handling peppers provides extra protection.) *Serves 2*

4 large eggs
2–3 tablespoons milk, cream or half-
and-half
about 2 tablespoons unsalted butter
4 corn tortillas, warmed
salsa (below)
4 tablespoons sour cream at room tem-
perature for garnish

Beat the eggs vigorously with the milk, cream or half-and-half. Heat the butter in a frying pan and scramble the eggs over medium-low heat, using a rubber spatula to turn and constantly move the eggs around. The consistency of the eggs should be smooth and creamy. Spoon the eggs over the warm corn tortillas and top with the salsa and sour cream.

SALSA

½ cup chopped fresh cilantro
2 medium tomatoes, seeded and chopped
1 jalapeño pepper, finely chopped (or
less, if you like a milder salsa)
½ large white onion, chopped
juice of ½ lemon

Mix together all the ingredients. Serve at room temperature or store in the refrigerator for up to 2 days.

**Huevos Rancheros
with Jalapeño
Cornbread**

THE ASPEN TIMES

Railroad plan
generates rift

Grande trail is key to
red citizen opposition

Parsi Scrambled Eggs

This recipe originated in India and made its way through the Middle East and finally to me in Colorado, courtesy of an Iranian friend. I serve it as a fancy brunch dish, or sometimes as a Sunday breakfast in bed. *Serves 4*

3 bananas
1 tablespoon unsalted butter, melted
3 tablespoons unsalted butter or
    vegetable oil
4 scallions, chopped
1 shallot, chopped
½ small jalapeño pepper, finely
    chopped
1 large tomato, chopped
2 teaspoons fresh mango, chopped
2 tablespoons chopped fresh cilantro, or
    ½ teaspoon powdered coriander
½ teaspoon curry powder
¼ teaspoon turmeric
salt
8 eggs
2 tablespoons whipping cream

Preheat broiler.

Peel the bananas and halve them lengthwise. Place them in a small, heatproof buttered dish and brush them with the melted butter. Broil for a few minutes until lightly browned. Remove and keep hot.

Place the 3 tablespoons butter or oil in a large sauté pan over medium heat. When the butter starts to foam, add the chopped scallions and stir for a few minutes. Add the chopped shallot and cook until the mixture is golden but not brown. Lower heat and stir in the jalapeño, tomato, mango, cilantro or powdered coriander, curry powder and turmeric. Mix well, add salt to taste and cook over low heat for 3 to 4 minutes. Remove from heat.

In a bowl, whisk together the eggs and cream until frothy. Return pan to heat and pour in the eggs. Stir over low heat until the eggs are creamy (don't overcook). Serve with the hot bananas.

French Toast with Brandied Lemon Butter

I love French toast only if it is made with great bread. Let's face it, that's the most important ingredient. Buy an uncut loaf—white, sourdough, wheat, even raisin—from a good bakery. Or have the baker slice it, at least an inch thick. The bread should be a day or two old; if the loaf is fresh, simply spread the slices out on the kitchen counter and let them dry overnight, turning once.

The brandied lemon butter in this recipe is extremely festive and a nice change of pace from maple syrup. *Serves 6*

---

4 eggs
2 tablespoons + 1 teaspoon white sugar
½ teaspoon salt
1 cup whole milk
¼ teaspoon Vanilla Extract (commercial or page 11)
6 thick slices day-old bread
4 tablespoons unsalted butter
Brandied Lemon Butter (below)
lemon slices for garnish

In a shallow dish, beat together the eggs, sugar, salt, milk and vanilla. Soak the bread on both sides in the egg mixture.

Melt the butter in a large skillet over medium-high heat. Add the bread and cook until lightly browned, then turn and brown the other side. (You may have to fry the bread in two batches or in two skillets at the same time.) Serve with maple syrup or, for a fancy breakfast, with Brandied Lemon Butter, garnished with lemon slices.

BRANDIED LEMON BUTTER

1/2 cup unsalted butter
1 cup white sugar
1 tablespoon + 1 teaspoon grated
*   lemon rind (no white pith)*
juice of 2 lemons
3 ounces brandy or rum

In a medium saucepan over low heat, melt the butter. Blend in the sugar, stirring constantly. Stir in the grated lemon rind. Add the lemon juice and brandy and stir until smooth. Pour over hot French toast.

Open-Faced Omelet Paysanne

This omelet works for me only if I use a non-stick pan. It is extremely hearty, great for a cold morning of skiing or wood chopping. I've been tempted to rename it the "skier's breakfast." *Serves 1*

½ potato, *diced*
3–4 tablespoons unsalted butter
½ medium white onion, chopped
2 strips bacon
2 eggs
1–2 tablespoons milk or cream
chopped chives for garnish
freshly ground black pepper for garnish

Fry the potatoes in a little of the butter in a non-stick pan over medium heat until browned and cooked through. Drain on paper towels and keep hot. Add the onion and sauté over low heat until lightly colored and soft. Drain on paper towels and keep hot. Fry the bacon over medium-high heat until crisp, drain on paper towels, and keep hot with the potatoes and onions.

Beat the eggs vigorously with a little milk or cream. Put a pat of the remaining butter in a clean non-stick frying pan and place over medium heat. When the butter begins to foam, pour in the eggs. Put the onions and potatoes on top of the cooking eggs and, with a fork, move the wet eggs around a little to lightly cover the onions and potatoes with eggs. Continue cooking for a moment more, until the eggs are done to your taste, then place the bacon strips on top and slide the open-faced omelet onto a plate. Garnish with a sprinkling of the chopped chives and some fresh black pepper. Serve at once.

Oeufs Estragon

This recipe for *oeufs estragon*, or eggs tarragon, was given to me by the owners of the Chlosterli restaurant in Gstaad, Switzerland. They serve two eggs for lunch; for breakfast I prefer only one. *Serves 1*

1–2 tablespoons whipping cream
1 or 2 eggs
pinch dried tarragon
freshly grated nutmeg to taste

Preheat oven to 350°F.

Pour a little of the cream into the bottom of a small ramekin or oven-proof custard cup. Break 1 or 2 eggs into the cup and top with enough cream to cover. Sprinkle a pinch of tarragon into the cream and top with a small sprinkling of freshly grated nutmeg.

Place the cup into a deep pan filled with enough boiling water to come halfway up the sides of the cup. Bake for 5 to 10 minutes, or until the whites have solidified but the yolk is not hard. Serve at once.

Ricotta Cheese Pancakes

Serves 6

1 cup all-purpose flour
1 teaspoon baking powder
1 teaspoon sugar
¼ teaspoon salt
1 pound ricotta cheese
2 whole eggs
2 egg yolks
⅔ cup half-and-half
1 tablespoon unsalted butter, melted
Cranberry Butter (opposite)

Into a large mixing bowl, sift together the flour, baking powder, sugar and salt. Add the ricotta cheese and blend well.

In a separate bowl, beat the whole eggs with the egg yolks, half-and-half and melted butter.

Place a griddle or skillet over medium-high heat and butter it. Drop spoonfuls of the batter onto the hot griddle and cook until lightly browned. Turn and brown on the other side. Serve with Cranberry Butter, syrup or jam.

Cranberry Butter

Makes about 1 cup

¹/₃ pound (5¹/₃ ounces) cranberries
1¹/₂ cups powdered sugar
¹/₂ cup unsalted butter
1 teaspoon ground ginger
1 tablespoon fresh lemon juice

Put all the ingredients into a blender or food processor fitted with the steel blade and blend or process until smooth. Chill.

Serve with pancakes, waffles, French toast, toast or muffins.

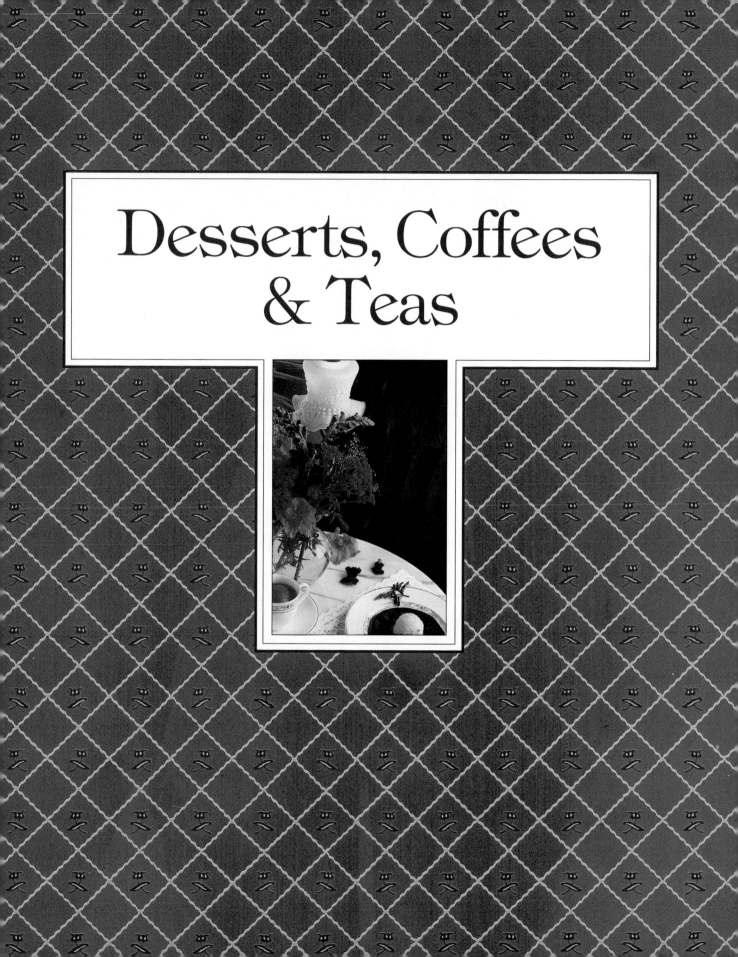

Desserts, Coffees
& Teas

When I was a child, I couldn't understand why I had to wait until the end of the meal for dessert —clearly the best part of dinner. As an adult, of course, I understand. But being an actress, I tend to go for the grand finale, with favorites like my Ruby & Sapphire Pudding or Blueberry Pavlova. Dessert and a flavored coffee or tea makes a meal memorable.

You may notice that most all of my recipes incorporate nature's dessert, fruit. If you don't have time or don't want to trouble yourself with cooking a dessert, peel and slice a perfectly ripe fruit, sprinkle it with a liqueur such as kirsch, and enjoy. But do flavor your coffee. It's no trouble at all. Your guests will be delighted by a hint of cinnamon-vanilla, anise or cardamom, to mention a few. Instead of decaf, offer my *cannerino* or crème de menthe tea. Those small finishing touches mean a lot.

Peppermint Mousse and Peppermint Ice Cream with Chocolate Sauce and Crème de Menthe Tea

Peppermint Mousse

Serves 8

1/2 pound red and white peppermint
   candies
1/2 cup half-and-half
1 tablespoon cold water
2 teaspoons unflavored gelatin
1 1/2 cups whipping cream
2–3 drops red food coloring
Chocolate Sauce (below)
fresh mint sprigs for garnish

In the work bowl of a food processor fitted with the steel blade, finely chop the peppermint candy. Transfer the candy to the top of a double boiler set over simmering water. Add the half-and-half and stir until the candy dissolves.

Put the cold water into a cup, sprinkle in the gelatin and stir. Stir the gelatin into the peppermint mixture until the gelatin dissolves. Remove from heat and allow to cool.

Whip the cream with the red food coloring until stiff and fold it into the peppermint mixture. Pour into a 4-cup mold and chill in the fridge until firm.

To unmold, run a small, sharp knife around the edge, immerse very briefly in hot water, and invert on a large, chilled platter. Garnish with the fresh mint sprigs and serve with the chocolate sauce.

Lemon Sorbet

This is the freshest-tasting lemon sorbet I know. It's a perfect way to end a heavy meal or to highlight a light one.
Makes about 1 quart

1 cup sugar
1 cup water
grated rind of 2 lemons (no white pith)
2¼ cups fresh lemon juice
2 egg whites
Raspberry Sauce (opposite)

In a saucepan, combine the sugar and water and place over medium heat, stirring constantly until sugar is dissolved. Remove from heat just as the mixture is coming to a boil. Transfer to a bowl and set the bowl in a basin or sink of cold water. When cool, cover and refrigerate for 1 hour.

Add the grated lemon rind and lemon juice to the cold syrup. Pour into an ice cream maker and freeze according to the manufacturer's instructions until it is half frozen.

Open canister, remove paddle and scrape mixture into a food processor fitted with the plastic or steel blade. Pulse on and off until the mixture is fluffy. Add egg whites and process until completely blended. Return to canister and freeze until set. Serve with the Raspberry Sauce.

Raspberry Sauce

Another quickie—we can all use those once in a while. Serve with ice creams, sorbets, fruits, tarts or anything lemony. *Makes about 2 cups*

a 10-ounce package frozen raspberries with sugar added

Defrost raspberries, purée in blender, strain and serve.

Lemon Sorbet with Raspberry Sauce and *Cannerino*

Ruby & Sapphire Pudding

This is the best (and prettiest) dessert I have ever made. The color depends on the fruits. I try to use mostly red fruits for a "ruby" pudding; that way the blueberry "sapphires" provide more of a contrast. *Serves 12*

1 loaf sliced day-old white bread
2 cups superfine sugar
2 cups red currants
2 cups hulled and halved strawberries
2 cups blackberries or boysenberries
2 cups raspberries
1 cup blueberries for garnish
edible flowers for garnish

Remove the crusts from the bread. Cut a round of bread to fit the bottom of a large pudding mold or other deep bowl and fit it in place. Then line the inside of the bowl with bread slices, trimming as necessary.

In a stainless steel or enameled saucepan, mix together the sugar and red currants and cook for 4 minutes. Add the strawberries and cook for 1 minute. Add the blackberries or boysenberries and cook 1 minute more. Add the raspberries, stir and remove from heat. Taste and add more sugar if necessary. Drain the fruit, reserving the juice.

When the fruit has cooled, spoon it into the bread-lined bowl, tamping it down with the back of a large spoon. When you have packed in all the fruit, pour in the reserved juice. Cover the fruit with slices of the bread cut to fit exactly. Cover with a plate small enough to fit on top of the pudding itself. Place some heavy cans or other weights on top of the plate and refrigerate overnight.

Remove the weights and plate and gently loosen the edges of the pudding with a knife. Invert on a large plate deep enough to hold the juices. Decorate with the blueberries and edible flowers. Serve with vanilla ice cream or sweetened whipped cream.

Chocolate Sauce

I much prefer using raw sugar in this recipe as it gives the chocolate a more interesting flavor. The sauce is good over almost any dessert: ice cream, mousses and fruits, like bananas and berries. Or, if you are truly sinful, have a spoonful on its own.

1 cup water
½ cup raw sugar
4 ounces unsweetened chocolate

Place the water and sugar in a medium saucepan over medium heat and stir often until it comes to a boil. While you are stirring, dip a pastry brush into cold water and brush down the sides of the pan to keep the sugar from crystallizing.

Melt the chocolate in the top of a double boiler placed over simmering water. Stir in the sugar syrup, mix until smooth and remove from heat. Serve warm or at room temperature.

Cinnamon-Coffee Ice Cream

Makes about 1½ quarts

4 cups half-and-half
⅔ cup freshly ground French roast
  coffee beans
¾ cup sugar
1–2 teaspoons cinnamon
pinch salt
2 teaspoons Vanilla Extract
  (commercial or page 11)

In a medium saucepan, mix the half-and-half with the ground coffee and scald over medium heat. Add the sugar, cinnamon to taste and salt. Pour into a bowl set in a basin or sink of cold water. Let cool.

Stir in the Vanilla Extract. Chill in the fridge, covered, for 1 hour, then freeze according to the manufacturer's instructions.

Cinnamon-Coffee Ice
Cream with Cinnamon-
Vanilla Coffee

Peppermint Ice Cream

Making ice cream in an electric or hand-cranked freezer is fairly simple. Follow the manufacturer's instructions, but if you have misplaced them, here's how I do it:

Fill the canister no more than three-quarters full with the ice cream base, to allow for expansion. As the machine is cranked, the paddles incorporate air into the custard, making it smooth and soft enough to scoop while frozen.

Place the filled canister into the freezing unit and pack it with alternating layers of four parts shaved ice and one part rock salt or kosher salt (available in most markets).

Some recipes call for the addition of fruits, nuts, cookies or candy when the ice cream base is half frozen. Remove the canister very carefully to prevent any salt from getting inside. Lift out the dasher, add the new ingredients and replace the dasher and lid. Repack with salt and ice as before and continue cranking. When the crank absolutely refuses to turn, the ice cream is done.

Remove canister and wipe away salt and ice. Now test your willpower. For the best flavor, ice cream should "mellow" for 5 to 6 hours or overnight in the freezer.

Scrupulously clean your ice cream freezer before storing as the salt is highly corrosive to the metal.

Now dig in and enjoy! *Makes 1½ pints*

━━━━━━━━━━━━━━━━━━━━━━━━━━━━━━━━━━━━

2 eggs
2 egg yolks
4 tablespoons white sugar
1¼ cups whole milk
1¼ cups whipping cream
2 tablespoons peppermint schnapps or white crème de menthe
2–3 drops red food coloring
4 tablespoons crushed red and white peppermint candy, crushed
Chocolate Sauce (page 238)

With a portable electric hand mixer, beat the eggs and the egg yolks in a large bowl until they start to foam. Add the sugar and beat until the mixture is thick and fluffy.

Heat a large pot of water just to the boiling point and hold at a simmer. In a saucepan, heat the milk to just short of boiling, then pour it into the eggs, beating constantly. When the eggs and milk are thoroughly mixed, set the bowl over the pot of simmering water. With a wooden spoon, stir the egg and milk mixture for 7 or 8 minutes, or just until it thickens enough to coat the spoon.

(Do not let it boil, or the eggs will curdle.) Remove from heat.

Using a metal sieve, strain the custard into a large bowl and set the bowl in a sink or basin of very cold water. Either cover the surface with a round of waxed paper cut to fit, or stir frequently to prevent a skin from forming as it cools.

Whip the cream to stiff peaks and fold into the cooled custard. Fold in the schnapps or crème de menthe and the red food coloring.

Pour the mixture into your ice cream maker and freeze according to the manufacturer's directions, until the ice cream is half frozen.

Carefully open the canister, remove the paddle and stir in the crushed peppermint candy. Replace the paddle and canister and continue freezing until set. Serve with the Chocolate Sauce.

Fresh Fruit Tart with Pecan or Almond Crust

Choose your fruits with an eye to color. I like kiwis, strawberries, raspberries and bananas. (If using bananas, drizzle with lemon juice to prevent discoloration.) *Makes one 8- or 9-inch tart*

1 cup cold heavy whipping cream (36–40 percent butterfat)

5 teaspoons powdered sugar

1½ teaspoons Vanilla Extract (commercial or page 11)

1 Pecan or Almond Tart Crust (opposite)

about 2 cups assorted fresh fruit

Chill a large mixing bowl and the whisk or beater you intend to use to whip the cream, in the freezer for 20 to 30 minutes. Whisk or beat the cold cream until it forms soft mounds. Gradually whisk or beat in the powdered sugar and the Vanilla Extract and continue to whip until the cream is stiff. (Stop beating at this point or you will make butter almost immediately.) With a spatula, spread the cream over the cooled crust. Top with a decorative layer of sliced fresh fruit of your choice.

Pecan or Almond Tart Crust

This is an all-purpose tart crust. The nuts make it special, and using them eliminates about a cup of flour. I usually fill the shell with whipped cream and fresh fruit. However, a filling of custard, lemon meringue or chiffon also goes well with a nut crust. *Makes two 8- or 9-inch tart crusts*

12 ounces pecans or almonds, very
    finely chopped
1 cup + 1 tablespoon unsalted butter
½ cup sugar
3¼ cups all-purpose flour
1 large or 2 small egg(s)
1½ teaspoons Vanilla Extract (com-
    mercial or page 11)

Butter two 8- or 9-inch tart pans.

In a large mixing bowl, combine all the ingredients with an electric or hand mixer until well-blended.

Divide the dough in half and press evenly into the buttered tart pans. Refrigerate for 30 minutes to 1 hour.

Preheat oven to 350°F.

Bake on the middle rack of the oven for 25 minutes, or until the crusts are golden brown. Allow to cool completely on a rack before removing from pan and filling as desired.

Terrine of Fresh Fruit with Raspberry Sauce

Summer offers us so many glorious fruits that they deserve this regal setting. But don't cheat on the recipe by using Jell-O. It won't taste the same, it won't look the same and I won't like you anymore. I'm leaving the tartness of the limeade or lemonade up to you. I make mine very tart as I feel that shows off the other fruit flavors best. My favorite fruits for the terrine are sliced nectarines, papayas, mangos, bananas, strawberries, peaches and pears. To fill the spaces in the fruit layers, I use halved red and green seedless grapes as well as blueberries, blackberries, raspberries and my favorite California berry, the boysenberry. *Serves 6–8*

½ cup water

1 tablespoon + ½ teaspoon unflavored gelatin

1½ cups tart fresh limeade or lemon-ade, strained

3 cups assorted fresh berries or chopped or sliced fruit (any combination will do, except do not use fresh or frozen pineapple or kiwis)

Raspberry Sauce (page 235)

In a small saucepan, bring the water to a boil and stir in the gelatin. When the gelatin has completely dissolved, remove from heat and allow to cool slightly. Stir in the lime- or lemonade.

Fill a large, deep-sided baking pan with ice and add water to fill halfway. Place a 6-cup non-stick loaf pan in the center of the baking pan. Pour about ¼ inch of the lime or lemon gelatin into the loaf pan and allow to set (about 15 minutes). Add a tight layer of one kind of fruit. Coat the fruit with a little more gelatin and then cover with a layer of another fruit. (Sliced seedless red or green grapes, blueberries, blackberries and boysenberries are good for filling any empty pockets.) Cover with another layer of gelatin, adding more ice to the baking pan as needed. Allow to set and then arrange more layers of fruit and gelatin, allowing each to set before forming a new one. Finish with a ¼-inch layer of gelatin. Refrigerate 8 hours or overnight.

When ready to serve, dip the loaf pan into a basin or sinkful of warm water for several seconds, then slide a thin knife around the edge of the pan. Invert the terrine onto a serving platter, slice and serve with the Raspberry Sauce.

Blueberry Pavlova

An Australian original, this meringue shell filled with fruit and whipped cream was created in honor of the great balle-rina Anna Pavlova. They usually use blueberries Down Under, but any fresh fruit, alone or in combination, works. *Serves 10–12*

6 egg whites, *at room temperature*
¾ cup superfine sugar
2¼ teaspoons cornstarch
1¼ teaspoons Vanilla Extract (commercial or page 11)
1⅛ teaspoons white cider or malt vinegar
1½ cups whipping cream
1 tablespoon powdered sugar
2 pints blueberries or other berries of choice

Preheat oven to 300°F.

Using a 10- or 11-inch plate, trace a circle on a piece of baking parchment. Place the parchment on a baking sheet and set aside.

In a large, clean bowl, beat the egg whites until they form stiff peaks. Gradually add ½ cup of the sugar and continue to beat until the whites become shiny and stiff. Gently fold in the remaining sugar, the cornstarch, ¾ teaspoon of the vanilla and the vinegar.

Spoon one-third of the egg whites evenly over the circle you traced, being careful to stay within the border. Spoon the remaining egg whites into a pastry bag fitted with a plain 1-inch tip. Pipe decorative swirls or scallops along the edge of the circle to form a wall thick enough and high enough to hold the fruit; it should be about 1½ inches high.

Place the baking sheet on the middle shelf of the oven and bake for 65 minutes. Then turn the oven off and let the meringue continue to dry out in the oven until the shell is crisp on the outside but still soft inside (about 30 minutes). Remove the baking sheet from the oven and allow the meringue to cool.

Whip the cream with the powdered sugar and the remaining ½ teaspoon Vanilla Extract until stiff.

When the meringue is completely cool, carefully transfer it to a large platter and spoon two-thirds of the whipped cream into it. Pile the berries on top. Heap the rest of the whipped cream in the center and sprinkle with additional powdered sugar, if desired.

New Orleans Bananas

Inexpensive, flashy and quick, this dessert (also called Bananas Foster) has been a favorite in New Orleans for a hundred years. It's been one of *my* favorites for almost as long. *Serves 4*

4 bananas
3 tablespoons unsalted butter
5 tablespoons brown sugar
¼ cup fresh lemon juice
1 cup cinnamon
½ cup white rum

Peel the bananas and halve them lengthwise. In a chafing dish, melt the butter with the brown sugar. Stir in the lemon juice. Add the bananas and sauté until they are tender. Sprinkle with the cinnamon. Warm the rum and slowly pour it over the bananas. Set it alight and keep spooning the flaming rum over the bananas until the flame burns out. (The flames can be quite high, so pay attention.)

Serve hot, with scoops of French vanilla ice cream.

Crème de Menthe Tea

In Aspen I grow masses of mint. I inherited the plants from the former owners of my "ranchette." Unable to get rid of it (as all gardeners know), I've always had plenty without really trying. Peppermint makes a good tea, and a slug of crème de menthe or peppermint schnapps makes a great tea. *Makes 1 quart*

4 cups water
1 cup fresh mint leaves
4 tablespoons green crème de menthe

Bring the water to a boil and pour over the mint leaves. Cover and allow to steep for 1 hour. Reheat and strain into cups; add 1 tablespoon of the crème de menthe to each. (You may, alternatively, use dried mint tea bags, one per cup.)

Cannerino

It was wintertime in Venice, Italy, when I first encountered *cannerino*. It is wintertime in Venice, Italy, as I write these words. It is cold, 35 degrees. It rained yesterday and the Piazza San Marco is partially flooded by the high tide. The magical quality of this canal city seems heightened by the cold. I have ordered a *cannerino* to warm and soothe me. It has no caffeine and no calories. *Serves 1*

1 lemon
1 cup water

Using a sharp paring knife, carefully pare the lemon, trying to keep the peel in one piece. Place the peel in an individual cup or preheated teapot. Bring the water to a boil, pour over the peel, and allow to steep for about 5 minutes. Serve without removing the peel.

Cardamom Coffee

Flavored coffees are an ideal way to end a special dinner. I love to experiment with new flavors. One evening in Gstaad, Switzerland, at the home of some Egyptian friends, we were served an incredible feast of Egyptian dishes. The after-dinner coffee was redolent of cardamom. That amazing combination I now offer you. *Serving depends on quantity of ingredients*

whole cardamom pods
good-quality ground coffee

Place 3 whole cardamom pods per cup over good ground coffee and perk or brew using your own method.

Cinnamon-Vanilla Coffee

〰〰〰〰〰〰〰〰〰〰〰〰〰〰〰〰〰〰〰〰〰〰〰〰〰〰〰

This cinnamon-vanilla coffee combination was given to me by my cousin Nancy, who got it from her mother, Frances, who probably got it from my aunt Molly. It's fun to trace the progress of a recipe through the generations. *Serves 12*

〰〰〰〰〰〰〰〰〰〰〰〰〰〰〰〰〰〰〰〰〰〰〰〰〰〰〰

¼–½ teaspoon ground cinnamon
2-inch piece of vanilla bean, split
enough good-quality ground coffee for
  12 cups

Place the cinnamon and vanilla bean over the ground coffee. Brew or perk using your own method.

Anise Coffee

〰〰〰〰〰〰〰〰〰〰〰〰〰〰〰〰〰〰〰〰〰〰〰〰〰〰〰

Serves 10

½ teaspoon ground anise seed
enough good-quality ground coffee for
  10 cups

Place the anise seed over the ground coffee. Perk or brew in your usual way.

Chocolate Coffee

Serves 6

3/4 teaspoon cinnamon
3 tablespoons unsweetened cocoa powder
3 tablespoons sugar
1 1/2 tablespoons water
1 cup milk
1 1/2 ounces semisweet chocolate, cut into
    very small pieces
4 cups strong, hot coffee
6 tablespoons whipped cream, sweetened
    with 1 teaspoon powdered sugar
1 tablespoon grated semisweet chocolate
dusting of cinnamon for garnish

In a medium saucepan placed over low heat, stir together the cinnamon, cocoa, sugar and water for a minute or two. Slowly add the milk and beat or whisk the mixture until it is completely combined. Add the chocolate pieces and beat until they are completely melted and mixed in.

Divide the mixture equally among 6 tall cups; fill to the brim with hot coffee. Garnish with a dollop of the sweetened whipped cream and the grated chocolate. Top with a fine dusting of cinnamon.

INDEX

ABOUT THE AUTHOR

JILL ST. JOHN, the celebrated film and television star, is as comfortable in the kitchen as she is on a movie set. Her regular monthly cooking segments on ABC TV's *Good Morning America* have made her one of America's most watched television chefs. In addition, as one of *USA Weekend*'s food editors, she writes a popular column for the magazine on food and her own simple, stylish approach to contemporary dining.

Jill St. John has been acting since the age of four. As a leading lady, she has starred with Frank Sinatra, Dean Martin, Sean Connery, and Oliver Reed, among others. Bob Hope recognized her gift for comedy and had her under contract for seven years.

In addition to being a culinary expert, Jill St. John is a professional photographer and a practicing orchidologist as well as an avid gardener. She resides in Aspen, Colorado, and Beverly Hills, California. She enjoys skiing, hiking, river rafting and camping in between acting stints all over the world.

ABOUT THE PHOTOGRAPHER

David Marlow first visited Aspen as a child and has lived there for seventeen years, most of that time as a highly regarded commercial photographer. His photographs have been published in *Better Homes and Gardens*, *House Beautiful*, *Designer West* and *Architectural Record*, and can be seen each year in the Aspen, Santa Fe, Carmel and Miami catalogs. David lives with his wife, Connie, and their three children and four horses just outside Aspen in Old Snowmass, Colorado. After he had photographed Jill St. John for the covers of *Aspen* and *Electricity* magazines, Jill knew that he was the only one she wanted to photograph this book.